ELITE SERIES

EDITOR: MARTIN WINDROW

The Vikings

Text by IAN HEATH

Colour plates by ANGUS McBRIDE

OSPREY PUBLISHING LONDON

Published in 1985 by
Osprey Publishing Ltd
59 Grosvenor Street, London W1X 9DA
© Copyright 1985 Osprey Publishing Ltd
Reprinted 1985, 1986, 1987, 1988 (twice)

British Library Cataloguing in Publication Data

Heath, Ian,
   The Vikings.—(Elite; 3)
   1. Northmen   2. Vikings
   I. Title   II. Series
   948'.02   DL65

   ISBN 0-85045-565-0

Filmset in Great Britain
Printed in Hong Kong

Artist's Note

Readers may care to note that the original paintings
from which the colour plates in this book were
prepared are available for private sale. All
reproduction copyright whatsoever is retained by the
publisher. All enquiries should be addressed to:
   Scorpio Gallery
   50 High Street
   Battle
   Sussex   TN33 0EN

The publishers regret that they can enter into no
correspondence upon this matter.

The Vikings

Who were the Vikings?

'789: In this year King Beorhtric took to wife Eadburh, daughter of King Offa. And in his days there came for the first time three ships of Northmen, from Hörthaland: and the reeve rode thither and tried to compel them to go to the royal manor—for he did not know what they were—and they slew him. These were the first ships of the Danes to come to England.'

Thus the *Anglo-Saxon Chronicle* reports the first raid, and the first victim, of the Vikings. Four years later, in AD 793, there followed the much more famous raid on the island monastery at Lindisfarne: 'The harrying of the heathen miserably destroyed God's church in Lindisfarne by rapine and slaughter.' 'Never before has such terror appeared in Britain as we have now suffered from a pagan race,' wrote the contemporary scholar Alcuin, 'nor was it thought possible that such an inroad from the sea could be made. Behold the church of St Cuthbert, spattered with the blood of the priests of God, despoiled of all its ornaments; a place more venerable than any other in Britain has fallen prey to pagans.'

To the Anglo-Saxons, then, the Vikings were 'pagans', 'Danes' or 'Northmen', the term Viking itself being rarely used in sources outside of Scandinavia (even though it has been suggested by some scholars that the word derives from Saxon *wic*, a military encampment). Frankish sources too refer to them as *Nordmanni* (Northmen or Normans); while German chroniclers describe them as *Ascomanni* ('Ashmen', an unexplained description which, it has been suggested, may have derived from some of their ships being constructed of ash trees, even though most were of oak). Spanish Moslem sources refer to them as *al-Madjus* ('heathen wizards'); Slavic sources as *Rus* (possibly from the Finnish name for Sweden, *Rotsi*); and

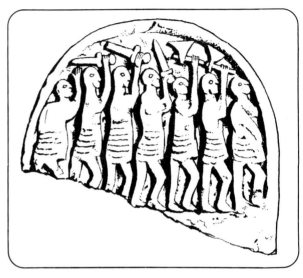

Vikings, from a tombstone at Lindisfarne monastery, doubtless erected over the grave of a victim of one of their raids.

Byzantine sources as *Rhos* (from the Greek adjective for red, because of their ruddy complexions) or *Varangoi* (probably from Old Norse *var*, 'pledge', describing a band of men who had sworn loyalty to one another). Only the Irish, who referred to them as *Lochlannach* ('Northerners') or *Gaill* ('strangers' or 'foreigners'), actually attempted to distinguish between Norwegians (*Finn-gaill*, 'white foreigners') and Danes (*Dubh-gaill*, 'black foreigners'), chroniclers of other nations tending to use the terms 'Danes', 'Norwegians', and even 'Swedes', interchangeably. For example, Adam of Bremen, writing *c*.1075, refers to 'the Danes and the Swedes whom we call Norsemen or Northmen'; and also tells us that 'the Danes and the Swedes and the other peoples beyond Denmark [i.e., the Norwegians] are called Norsemen'. Therefore when the *Anglo-Saxon Chronicle* repeatedly refers to *Dene* or *Dani*, it should not be assumed that the Vikings in question necessarily originated in Denmark.

The actual origin of the word 'Viking' is not known with absolute certainty, though there are a

The lid of the Franks Casket, produced in Northumbria in the early 8th century. Though pre-Viking, it is easy to imagine that scenes like this, of a man defending his house against armed raiders, were commonplace from the late 8th century onwards. (The Trustees of the British Museum)

growing number of scholars who favour a derivation from *vik* (an inlet, fjord or bay), which would make a Viking 'a pirate hidden in a fjord or inlet'. Other suggestions derive it from the geographical region of Vik in Norway; or else from *vig* (a battle, which is unlikely on phonological grounds); or from *vikja* (meaning to move or turn aside), making a Viking 'one who makes a detour'. In written Scandinavian sources *viking* actually means piracy or a pirate raid, while a man participating in such a foray was actually called a *vikingr*.

Suggested reasons for the sudden appearance of the Vikings at the end of the 8th century are many and varied. Overpopulation at home is usually cited as one of the prime factors, a population explosion having occurred in Norway and, more particularly, Denmark in the course of the 7th–8th centuries. In addition, the gradual establishment of firm government throughout much of Western Europe, especially on the Continent with the foundation of the Carolingian Empire under Charlemagne, had resulted in a considerable increase in European mercantile trade, which led in turn to increased opportunities for piracy. Undoubtedly connected with this was the stage of evolution that had been reached in the Scandinavian art of shipbuilding in the course of the 8th century. This had resulted not only in the justly famous longships which we invariably associate with the Vikings, but also in the

less well-known *knörrs*, or merchant vessels; in these respectively the Vikings were able to raid far afield and, subsequently, to colonise the lands they found. They were the very tools of Viking expansion.

Viking ships

Most of our knowledge of Viking ships has been gained from the discovery of two particular vessels buried in the second half of the 9th century at Gokstad and Oseberg in Norway. The ships unearthed at these famous sites are, however, only the most complete of a number of similar finds which have all added considerably to furthering our knowledge on the subject, the most recent being a group of five ships, of varying types, recovered in 1962 off Skuldelev in Roskilde Fjord, Zealand, where they had been sunk as blockships at the beginning of the 11th century. Most finds, however, have taken the form of ship-burials and have been found chiefly in Norway, only one such Viking-period discovery having been made in Denmark, at Ladby. The earliest to have been excavated successfully and preserved—somewhat less successfully—was that found at Tune in 1867, while those at Gokstad and Oseberg were excavated in 1880 and 1903 respectively.

Viking ships took many forms, as is apparent

Viking head, from a carving on the 9th-century Oseberg wagon frame. Like all surviving contemporary representations of Vikings, he is moustached and bearded. (Universitetets Oldsaksamling, Oslo)

from the profusion of technical terms used to describe them in contemporary sources; but a clear distinction between merchant vessels and warships seems to have evolved only in the 10th century (probably resulting not only from the growing importance of trade in the Scandinavian economy, but also from the establishment of *ledungen* military organisation, which required the construction of ships specifically for service in war). Amongst the terms most frequently encountered are: for merchant vessels, *knörr* and *kaupskip* ('trade-ship'); and for warships *snekkja* (meaning thin and projecting), *skeid* (probably meaning 'that which cuts through water'), and *drekar* or 'dragon', a term that undoubtedly evolved from the frequent use of a carved dragon-head on the prows of Viking warships. General-purpose vessels equally suited to both trade and piracy, such as that found at Gokstad, were usually described as *skuta* or *karfi*. The most distinct difference between merchant vessels and warships was that whereas the former were short and broad, with a high freeboard and a tendency to depend primarily on sail-power, warships were longer and thinner, drew little water (which increased their speed as well as enabling them to penetrate a long way upriver on their pirate expeditions), and had a greater number of oars. This resulted in the adoption of the generic term *langskip* or 'longship' to describe warships.

They varied considerably in size. Warships tended to be measured according to the number of rowing-places (*sessa*), or spaces between deck-beams ('rooms', *rum* or *spantrum*), that they contained. According to the 10th century Gulathinglaw a 13-bencher (*threttansessa*, i.e. a vessel with 13 benches on each side, or 26 oars in total) was the

The Oseberg ship *in situ* **during its excavation in 1904. Used as the burial ship for a Norwegian princess, it was built of oak and was 71 ft long. The mound heaped over it—originally nearly 20 ft high and over 120 ft in diameter—was largely of peat, which, with the subsoil of blue clay, aided in the preservation not just of its timbers and much of its equipment but also a wagon, four sledges, beds, and innumerable other everyday artefacts. (Universitetets Oldsaksamling, Oslo)**

smallest ship that could be 'counted by benches', which indicates that anything smaller was not considered suitable for war. We know that Viking ships used in raids on England in the late 9th century must have been of about 16 to 18 benches, as the *Anglo-Saxon Chronicle* tells us that the ships of 60 or more oars (i.e. 30 or more benches) built by King Alfred the Great of Wessex in 896 were 'almost twice as long' as those of the Vikings; certainly the Gokstad ship, belonging to about this date, was a 16-bencher. By the time the Gulathinglaw was set down the standard levy ship that could be called upon for military service was a 20- or 25-bencher; admittedly, levy ships of 30 benches could also be found, but only in very small numbers (the Gulathinglaw, for instance, records Norway's mid-10th century levy potential as 120 × 20-benchers, and 116 × 25-benchers, but only one 30-bencher).

Occasional giant warships of over 30 benches began to appear at the very end of the 10th century. King Olaf Tryggvasson's *Long Serpent* of 34 benches was the first and the most famous, probably being built in the winter of 998; but it was not, as many modern authorities assert, the largest ever built. This distinction would seem to belong to any one of the several 35-bench vessels recorded as having been built in the 11th–13th centuries, of which the first was King Harald Hardrada's *Great Dragon* constructed at Nidaros in the winter of 1061–1062.

The 9th-century Gokstad ship *in situ*, **Vestfold, Norway. It was excavated in 1880 from a burial mound 162 ft wide and 16 ft high where, again, blue clay had preserved it. (Universitetets Oldsaksamling, Oslo)**

King Harald's Saga describes how this 'was much broader than normal warships; it was of the same size and proportions as the *Long Serpent*, and each part was built with great care. On the stem was a dragon-head, and on the stern a dragon-tail, and the bows of the ship were gilded. It had 35 pairs of rowing benches, and was large [even] for that size and a magnificent vessel.' *Flateyjarbok* actually claims that King Cnut had a ship of as many as '60' rooms, but this is doubtless a mistake for 60 oars, since otherwise the vessel would have had to be an improbable—nay, impossible—230 ft or more in length.

The largest Viking ship that has been found so far is one of the five Skuldelev vessels: a warship in admittedly poor condition that has been estimated to have originally measured some 92 ft long and 15 ft wide, with probably between 20 and 25 benches. Of the other excavated examples, that at Ladby (*c*.900–950) was 70 ft long by 8½ ft wide—from its proportions clearly a warship, despite the fact that it

The carved prow of the Oseberg ship, ending in a spiral with, at its centre, a serpent's head. (Universitetets Oldsaksamling, Oslo)

had only 12 pairs of oars. That at Tune (*c*.850–900) was probably 65 ft long by 14½ ft wide with 11 pairs of oars; the Oseberg ship (*c*.800) was 71½ ft long by 17 ft wide with 15 pairs of oars (this was probably a sort of 'royal yacht'); and the Gokstad ship (*c*.850–900) was just over 76 ft long by 17½ ft wide with 16 pairs of oars. A *knörr* found at Skuldelev— the only one that has so far been discovered— measured 54 ft long by 15¾ ft wide.

Longships and general-purpose vessels had two small raised decks, at bow and stern, and between them a rough deck made up of loose planks that could be lifted to facilitate baling, which was continuously necessary in heavy weather. At anchor or in harbour the main deck area could be covered with a large awning over a collapsible, light timber framework, so as to provide the crew with some protection against the worst effects of the weather: *Svarfdaela Saga* records 12 ships at anchor 'all covered with black tents. Light came from under the tents, where the men sat drinking.' The crew's shields were often hung along the gunwales of this portion of the ship, though modern authorities frequently claim that this was only done 'on special occasions' and was not possible when the oars were in use. However, this view would appear to be based only on the evidence of the Gokstad ship, where the shields were tied by thongs through a batten so that they actually covered the oar-ports. On the Oseberg ship they were positioned instead in slots in a timber rail attached to the outside of the gunwale, in such a way that rowing was still possible; this tallies with the evidence of the sagas, which indicate that shields were sometimes arranged thus on ships being rowed into battle. At the Battle of Hafrs Fjord, for instance, the gunwales of the ships are described as 'glittering with burnished shields', and at the Battle of the River Nissa in 1062 'warriors made a bulwark of shields along the gunwales'. Gotland picture stones also depict shields displayed thus on ships under sail.

Curiously, there is no evidence of rowing benches in any of the Viking ships discovered to date, and therefore it is generally supposed that the seamen's chests must have doubled as seats (those found with the Oseberg ship being exactly the right height for

The Gokstad ship as reconstructed, in the Viking Ship Museum at Oslo. (Universitetets Oldsaksamling, Oslo)

GOKSTADSKIBET

rowing). However, several sources refer to seamen keeping their belongings not in chests but in skin kitbags, *hudfat*, which doubled as sleeping bags, so the seating question may not be so easily answered. In one of the Skuldelev warships it appears that the actual crossbeams may in fact have been used as seats, while one expert has even suggested that Viking oarsmen may have stood. The oars themselves usually averaged about 16–17 ft in length, those of the Gokstad ship being from 17 ft up to 19 ft 2 ins., the variation in length being designed to match the curvature of the ship's sides. Viking ships were normally rowed with only one man to an oar, but when battle was likely a second, and even a third man per oar might be taken on board to protect the oarsman from enemy missiles and provide a combat detail; doubtless these helped with the rowing before battle was joined. Olaf Tryggvasson's *Long Serpent* allegedly carried as many as eight men per half-room (i.e. per oar) at the Battle of Svöldr in 1000, as well as 30 other combatants; this would have given an unlikely complement of 574 men in all, which makes it more likely that there were eight men per room, not per half-room, which gives a total of 302 men.

For open sea voyages it was the large, square sail that provided motive power. This had been

Hugin, **a reconstruction of the Gokstad ship, built in Denmark and sailed across the North Sea in 1949. It is on permanent display in Pegwell Bay, near Ramsgate, Kent.**

adopted on Scandinavian vessels by the 8th century at the latest, and was doubtless one of the technological advances that helped bring about the Viking era. The *Viking*, a reconstruction of the Gokstad ship which was sailed across the Atlantic in 1893, achieved speeds of up to 11 knots under sail, taking just 28 days to reach Newfoundland from Bergen. Sails were probably made of wool, though some experts say they were of linen. The diamond and striped patterns on the sails of ships portrayed on Gotland picture stones probably represent strengthening strips of leather, rope or linen designed to prevent the woollen sails from losing their shape. The Gotland stones also appear to show an arrangement of reefing lines attached to the bottom of the sail which doubtless worked on the same principle as those employed on north Norwegian fishing boats up until the end of the 19th century—these bunched the sailcloth up between them when pulled, thereby taking in sail. The sagas describe Viking sails as striped or checkered in blue, red, green, and white, the remains of the Gokstad ship's sails having been white with red stripes. The mast was probably somewhat less than half the length of the ship in height, so that when lowered, as it was for battle, it would clear the beams in the stern. No complete masts have actually been found, however.

At the ship's stern, on the starboard ('steerboard') side, a large oar with a detachable tiller was

fitted, which served as a rudder. The stem and stern were usually carved to look like animal heads and tails, particularly those of dragons ('serpents')—a North European custom dating back to at least the 1st–2nd centuries AD, as is confirmed by Norwegian rock-carvings. Such figureheads, usually gilded, often gave ships their names: *Long Serpent*, *Bison*, *Crane* and *Man's Head* are just a few examples. Icelandic law required that ships' figureheads should be removed on approaching land lest the island's guardian spirits took flight. In fact this custom may have been universal among Scandinavians, since even the Bayeux Tapestry shows the Norman invasion fleet with figureheads whilst at sea, but without them once beached in England.

The Vikings Abroad

The Vikings in England: 9th–10th centuries

After the initial Viking attacks on England at the end of the 8th century there followed a period of relative calm, which was finally shattered some 40 years later when, in 835, the *Anglo-Saxon Chronicle* records that 'heathen men ravaged Sheppey'. Thereafter, for the rest of the century, hardly a year goes by without the *Chronicle* recording a Viking incursion somewhere in the country. At first these expeditions were no more than predatory raids launched during the summer months in search of booty and slaves, with no attempt being made at permanent settlement. In 850/851, however, there were signs of a change in strategy: the *Chronicle* reports under that year that 'for the first time, the heathen stayed through the winter', on the Isle of Thanet. In 855/856 a Viking host again 'stayed for the entire winter', this time on the Isle of Sheppey; in 864/865 Vikings again wintered on Thanet; and finally, in 865/866, a 'great fleet of pagans', having arrived from the Continent, wintered in East Anglia. This time the Vikings had come to stay.

The 'great fleet' that arrived in 865 included amongst its leaders several sons of the celebrated Danish king Ragnar Lodbrok ('Hairy-breeches'), who was regarded in the North as the very epitome of a true Viking. The sons in question were Ivar the Boneless, Halfdan, and Ubbi or Hubba, and *Ragnar's Saga* would have it that their attack was launched purely to avenge the alleged death in the

850s of their father at the hands of King Aella of Northumbria, who was supposed to have had him cast into a snake-pit after capturing him in battle. Despite the fact that Aella had only come to power in 866 and Ragnar had in reality probably been killed by a Norse king in Ireland, it is undeniable that, after they had spent a year looting and gathering reinforcements in East Anglia, Ragnar's sons attacked and took York at the end of 867; and the next year captured and ritually executed Aella, subsequently overrunning much of Northumbria

Some 375 sandstone and limestone picture stones survive on the island of Gotland, Sweden, dating from the 5th century to the end of the 10th. The best generally belong to the 8th–9th centuries. This particular example, from Lärbro, depicts a fully-rigged longship in the bottom panel, and a battle-scene in the top one; between them is a procession of warriors approaching Valhalla. (Antikvarisk-Topografiska Arkivet, Stockholm)

and eastern Mercia (868). In 869 Ivar led part of the host back to East Anglia, where he defeated and captured King Edmund who, like Aella, was executed. (Though Edmund was also seemingly shot through with arrows, both kings were actually killed by being subjected to the gruesome 'blood-eagle' torture.[1]) Ivar subsequently disappears from the story (he seems to have removed to Ireland and conquered Dublin, where he probably died in 873); and Halfdan became the host's chief leader in his stead, being the foremost of the seven Viking commanders recorded at the Battle of Ashdown in 871, of whom the other six (a king and five *jarls*) were all killed in this celebrated Saxon victory. The English success was shortlived, however: a series of defeats followed at Basing, Meretun, Reading and Wilton, by the end of which King Alfred of Wessex was obliged to sue for peace, not least because a new army of Vikings, referred to as the 'summer army', had now arrived from the Continent to reinforce

[1] The living victim had a number of ribs chopped away from his spine, and his lungs pulled out through these massive wounds, to lie pulsing on his back like red wings until he died.

Halfdan, and had participated in the Saxon defeat at Wilton.

For the next few years the Vikings concentrated on securing their conquests in eastern and northern England. They briefly set up puppet kings in both Northumbria and Mercia (the last Saxon king of the latter fled in 874) before distributing these kingdoms among themselves in 876 and 877 respectively. Halfdan then followed in the footsteps of his brother Ivar, sailing to Ireland in a bid to secure for himself the kingdom of Dublin, only to be defeated and killed by Norwegian Vikings in the Battle of Strangford Lough (877).

This resulted in a certain Guthrum—who, with two other kings named Oskytel and Anwend, had commanded the 'summer army' of 871 (now based in Cambridge)—becoming the chief captain of the Danish host in England. In 878 Guthrum came within an ace of extinguishing the last independent Saxon kingdom: the *Anglo-Saxon Chronicle* reports how 'the host went secretly in midwinter . . . and rode over Wessex and occupied it, and drove a great

part of its inhabitants overseas, and reduced the greater part of the rest to submission, except Alfred the king; and he with a small company moved under difficulties through woods and into inaccessible places in marshes.' With Alfred still free, however, there was no chance for permanent Viking occupation. He struck out at the Viking invaders from a fortress he had established at Athelney—'surrounded by swampy, impassable and extensive marshland and groundwater on every side' and inaccessible except by boat—and soon afterwards, rallying the men of Somerset, Wiltshire and Hampshire, routed Guthrum at the Battle of Edington (Ethandun). As a result of this defeat Guthrum and the other Viking leaders were obliged to hand over hostages, embrace Christianity and leave Wessex.

A somewhat later peace treaty drawn up between Alfred and Guthrum in 886 effectively established the area of Danish occupation that was later (by the 11th century) to become known as the Danelaw, comprising East Anglia and the 'Five

Boroughs' of Derby, Leicester, Lincoln, Nottingham and Stamford. Evidence of the extent of Scandinavian settlement in this area can still be seen today in the number of place-names ending in -thorpe ('village'), -thwaite ('meadow') and -by ('farmstead').

The very same year another Viking host descended on England, but after wintering at Fulham understandably withdrew to the Continent, where they carved a trail of mayhem and destruction for more than a decade. In 892, however, following a defeat the previous year at the hands of Arnulf, king of Eastern Francia, this 'Great Army' returned to England, bringing with it from Boulogne its own horses. Several years of spasmodic fighting ensued throughout the length and breadth of Alfred's kingdom; but in the summer of 896 'the Viking army dispersed, some into East Anglia, some into Northumbria, and those who were without property got ships for themselves and went south across the sea to the Seine'. The fact that the last group sailed in just five ships, and therefore numbered no more than 350–400 men at most, would tend to confirm the view of various modern authorities that this so-called 'Great Army' may have consisted of no more than 1,000 men in all; some even believe it may have comprised just 500 men. (For myself, I cannot believe that it originally numbered less than 2,000–3,000.)

Even after the 'Great Army' had disbanded, the resident Vikings of East Anglia and Northumbria continued to harass Wessex by both land and sea. However, King Alfred, who died in 899, had left to his successors a strong, well-organised military establishment both on land and at sea with which Edward the Elder (899–925) and Athelstan (925–940) were able to reconquer the Danelaw.

This is one of the ornamental gilt copper or bronze vanes (*vedrviti*) that the sagas record to have been carried on the prows of many Viking longships as a sign of importance. Four examples have survived, as wind-vanes on church steeples: that depicted comes from Söderala, Hälsingland, Sweden while the others are from Källunge, Gotland and from Heggen and Tingelstad in Norway. All four probably date to the 11th–13th centuries, though the Söderala example is sometimes assigned to the 10th century. The Heggen example at least has several scratches and dents, thought to have been caused by arrows. Such vanes remained in use for as long as Viking-style longships did, and probably found their way on to church steeples as a result of the traditional practice of stowing the sails and other movable items of levy ships' equipment in local churches. After a disastrous 15th-century sea-battle against a Hansa fleet of high-sided cogs the old longships were never again levied; their equipment was probably thrown out, and the churches thereby inherited the *vedrviti*. (Antikvarisk-Topografiska Arkivet, Stockholm

The drawing is taken from an incised stick of the first half of the 13th century found at Bergen, depicting the prows of a Norwegian fleet of which three vessels are equipped with vanes.

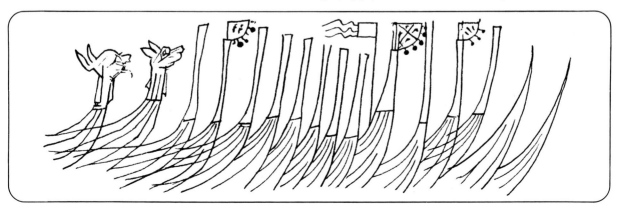

9th- and 10th-century Norwegian weapons: a Gokstad shield, the Gjermundbu helmet, and swords, spearheads and axeheads from various sites. (Universitetets Oldsaksamling, Oslo)

Northumbria held out somewhat longer, partly due to the influx of a new wave of Viking invaders—this time Norsemen from Ireland, who captured York from the Danes in 919, and established their own dynasties there which were accepted by Scandinavian settlers and Northumbrian Saxons alike. At one time or another, they also ruled over the Norse settlements of Ireland, the Western Isles and the Orkneys, as well as the Five Boroughs. Nevertheless, King Rognvald of York acknowledged South

Saxon suzerainty as early as 920, as did King Sihtric in 926; and in 927 Athelstan marched on York and evicted Sihtric's son and successor Olaf, and his brother, Olaf's mentor and regent, Guthfrith. However, the latter's own son, another Olaf, recaptured York before the end of 939 and the very next year received the Five Boroughs by treaty. He was succeeded as king of York by his less vigorous cousin Olaf Sihtricsson (who had been thrown out in 927), from whom the South Saxons were able to retake the Five Boroughs in a single decisive campaign in 942, Olaf himself being expelled in 944.

Olaf made at least one comeback, in 949–952,

but the dubious distinction of being the last Viking king of York undoubtedly belongs to a son of King Harald Fairhair of Norway, the celebrated Eric Bloodaxe, who has been described as 'the most famous Viking of them all'. He reigned in Northumbria twice, in 947–948 and 952–954. The *Anglo-Saxon Chronicle* states simply that in 954 'the Northumbrians drove Eric out' and that King Eadred of England thereby succeeded to the kingdom; but later Icelandic sagas, deriving their information from a lost 10th century Northumbrian chronicle, give a fuller account. According to them Eric was confronted at a place called Stainmore by 'King Olaf, a tributary king of King Edmund [sic]' who had 'gathered an innumerable mass of people, with whom he marched against King Eric. A dreadful battle ensued, in which many Englishmen fell; but for each one that fell there came three in his place from the country round about, and when evening came on the loss of men turned against the Northmen and many were killed. Towards the end of the day, King Eric and five kings with him fell. Three of them were Guttorm, Ivar and Harek [the last-named being one of his sons]; the others being Sigurd and Ragnvald [the latter one of his brothers] and with them died the two sons of Turf-Einar [the Earl of Orkney], Arnkel and Erlend.'

A much later English chronicle, probably working from the same lost account, would have it that Eric was in fact defeated and killed by a certain Maccus (Magnus), son of Olaf, rather than by Olaf himself, and it is likely—since his army comprised Englishmen—that the sagas' 'Olaf' is in fact an error for Oswulf, who was the Saxon earl of Bamburgh.

Either way, Eric was dead and the Viking kingdom of York at an end. 'From that time to the present,' wrote John of Wallingford, 'Northumbria has been grieving for want of a king of its own, and for the liberty they once enjoyed.'

The Vikings in Ireland: the Battle of Clontarf

Though it has been suggested that a fleet which raided the Hebrides and northern Ireland in 617 may actually have been Scandinavian, the first positively recorded Viking raid on Ireland dates to 795, when the island of Reachrainn (often identified with Lambey Island near Dublin, but more

9th-century sword, with the typical English style of curved hilt which in the 10th century was copied by the Vikings. Found at Abingdon in 1890. (Ashmolean Museum, Oxford)

15

probably Rathlin Island, five miles north-east of the Irish mainland) was plundered and two monasteries on the west coast were sacked. At first no more than hit-and-run affairs executed by small forces, these raids intensified after 830; and colonisation commenced *c*.840 with the arrival of a certain Turgesius, or Turgeis—a semi-legendary character who, according to the Irish chroniclers, made himself 'King of all the Foreigners in Erin'. Dublin was established at about this time when a *longphort* was constructed at a ford on the River Liffey, the Vikings first wintering there in 841–842. Before long similar Viking encampments and settlements had sprung up along much of Ireland's coastline and, further inland, along the courses of its navigable waterways—Cork, Limerick, Waterford, Wexford and Wicklow being the major examples (though most of these only became important in the 10th century). With the exception of just one brief

period in 902–919 Dublin was thereafter the seat of Viking power in Ireland under its own self-appointed kings.

One inevitable result of settling down in Ireland was that the Viking communities (mostly of Norsemen) soon found themselves being drawn into the unstable Irish political scene, where petty kings of minor kingdoms were almost continually at war with one another. Alliances between Vikings and Irishmen were, therefore, not uncommon after the mid-9th century, the Dublin Vikings even becoming traditional allies of the kings of Leinster. Indeed, it was this last alliance that in 1014 led to one of the most celebrated battles in Viking and Irish history, when the king of Dublin supported Máelmórdha of Leinster in his rebellion against the High King Brian Boru. The battle, of course, was Clontarf.

Brian Boru, a dynamic and ambitious chieftain, was one of the few High Kings of the medieval period who could with any justification claim to be king of Ireland in more than just name—an achievement which did not endear him to the country's many and fiercely independent petty dynasts. At the very end of the 10th century, in the closing months of 999, Máelmórdha of Leinster and King Sigtrygg Silkybeard of Dublin rose in revolt against Brian, who marched to meet them in the foothills of the Wicklow Mountains. He inflicted a crushing defeat on their combined forces at Glenn Máma, Máelmórdha only escaping the carnage by taking refuge in a yew tree. Although he and Sigtrygg were subsequently re-instated in their kingdoms by the magnanimous victor, their humiliation at Brian's hands was a festering wound which, according to one account, was tactlessly re-opened by Brian's hot-headed son Murchad in 1012. The story would have it that Murchad, beaten in a game of chess as a result of Máelmórdha giving advice to his opponent, cursed the king of Leinster, and observed that his advice was not always so fruitful: 'How wonderfully you advised the Norsemen that day they were smashed by us at Glenn Máma!' Deeply offended, Máelmórdha replied, 'I'll advise them again, but this time the outcome will be different'; to which Murchad retorted, 'Be sure to have a yew tree ready!'

Máelmórdha departed angrily from Brian's court, rallied his chieftains, and urged rebellion among the northern kings; by 1013 war had broken out in several quarters. However, Murchad soon had Máelmórdha on the run, and in the late summer he was obliged to take refuge with Sigtrygg in fortified Dublin. Here they were invested by Murchad and Brian until Christmas, when Brian's Munster army broke camp and dispersed for the winter. Making the most of this unexpected respite, Sigtrygg took ship for the North, sailing to the courts of the Viking-held Western Isles in search of allies. According to the *Annals of Innisfallen* he subsequently received troops from the *Gaill* or 'Foreigners' of the whole Western world, various accounts referring to Viking reinforcements arriving from the Hebrides, Caithness, Kintyre, Argyll, Norway and—more improbably—France, Flanders, Frisia and even Russia. Certainly Earl Sigurd the Stout of Orkney is known to have come to Sigtrygg's support, as did a certain Brodir of Man with 20 ships (though his partner Ospak, with another ten ships, joined Brian).

In the spring of 1014 all these forces assembled outside Dublin, where towards the end of April the High King confronted them with an army estimated at some 20,000 men drawn from Munster, the *Mide* ('Midlands') and southern Connacht. On 23 April—Good Friday—both sides drew up for battle on the plain of Clontarf.

There have been various attempts at establishing the dispositions of the two armies, few of them wholly convincing. However, scholars seem to fundamentally agree that the Vikings and their Leinster allies, drawn up in five or seven divisions, spread themselves too thin, in an effort to defend not only their line of retreat back into Dublin across a bridge over the Liffey, but also, on the opposite flank, to cover the ships of the foreign Vikings

Decorated Danish sword hilts. The large pommel served as a counterweight to the blade, making the sword easier to handle in the strenuous style of swordplay that prevailed in the Viking age. We are told that swordsmen 'did not strike fast and furiously, but took their time and picked their strokes carefully, so that they were few but terrible. More regard was given to the weight of each blow than to the number struck.' (Nationalmuseet, Copenhagen)

Viking warrior from a carved cross of the late 9th or early 10th century at Middleton, Yorkshire. Helmet, axe, sword, shield, spear and knife are all clearly visible.

forces is even more problematic. We know that their right flank was secured on the River Liffey, and their left on the parallel River Tolka. *Njal's Saga* says that the High King, now 73 years old, 'did not wish to wield weapons on Good Friday; so a wall of shields was formed round him and his army was drawn up in front of it'. Murchad was therefore in command, along with his cousin Conaing and 15-year-old son Toirdelbach; the saga also claims that Brian's youngest son Tadg was present. The 12th century *War of the Gaedhil with the Gaill*—which says that Brian stayed at prayer in his tent in Tomar's Wood—describes the Irish formation as a phalanx of men so tightly packed together that 'a four-horsed chariot could run from one end to the other of the line on their heads, so compact were they'; but it also mentions individual *battals*, or divisions, and three distinct lines.

'The armies clashed, and there was bitter fighting,' says *Njal's Saga*. In the centre of the line Máelmórdha led a downhill charge that drove deep into Murchad's ranks, but his Viking allies on either flank fared less well. After heavy fighting, Murchad's predominance in numbers—still apparent despite the withdrawal of the forces of *Mide* before the battle—began to prevail. The Leinstermen, having advanced too far unsupported, were driven back in disarray, as were the Vikings. The Dubliners on the right, falling back towards the town, were pursued so closely that allegedly only 20 men, or according to one version only nine, actually reached the fortress alive. The Viking left flank meanwhile rallied and the Leinstermen fell back on it; but they were now virtually encircled on both left and right by Murchad's victorious Munstermen. They had no choice but to retreat towards the sea, from which there was little hope of escape since high tide had put the Vikings' ships beyond reach of all but the strongest swimmers. Inevitably, therefore, a great many met their death by drowning.

However, despite the fact that some 12 hours of solid fighting had now elapsed, this was not quite the end of the battle. In their desperation some

anchored in Dublin Bay. *Njal's Saga* puts Brodir on one flank, King Sigtrygg on the other, and Earl Sigurd in the centre, but makes no mention of Máelmórdha or his Leinstermen despite the fact that they must have outnumbered the Viking element by at least two to one. It is in error, too, in assigning Sigtrygg a battlefield rôle, since he remained in Dublin throughout the battle, his brother Dubhgall commanding the Dublin contingent in his place. Probably the foreign Vikings under Sigurd and Brodir were mostly on the left flank in order to protect their ships, while the Dubliners guarded the bridge on the right, and Máelmórdha held the high ground commanding the centre of the line. The disposition of Brian's

A collection of 9th- and 10th-century Norwegian weapons and tools, including arrowheads, spearheads, and axeheads, a shield boss, stirrups and a horse bit. At top left is a *skeggox* or 'bearded axe'; the object at centre right is a *rangel*, a hollow iron mount attached to a ring, used as part of the steering traces of a wagon—the other rings served as a rattle, apparently to frighten away evil spirits which might otherwise dog a journey. (Universitetets Oldsaksamling, Oslo)

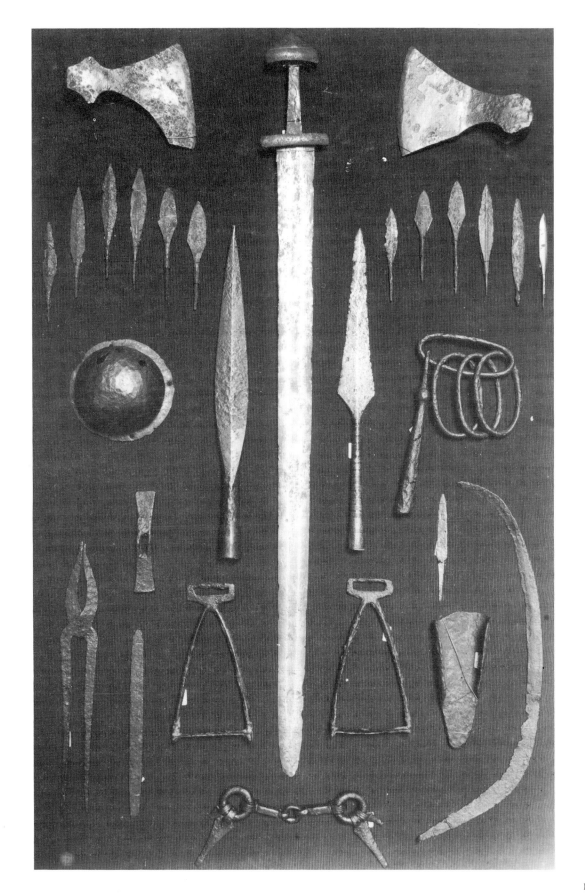

Vikings—Brodir among them—actually managed to hack through Murchad's army and reach the High King's encampment behind the Irish lines. 'Brodir could see that King Brian's forces were pursuing the fugitives,' says *Njal's Saga*, 'and that there were only a few men left to man the wall of shields. He ran from the woods and burst through the shield-wall and hacked at the king. The boy Tadg threw up an arm to protect Brian, but the sword cut off the arm and the king's head. . . . Then Brodir shouted, "Let the word go out that Brodir has felled Brian."' However, he had little time to enjoy his triumph, since he and his companions were surrounded and taken captive by the High King's bodyguards, and subsequently executed.

The *War of the Gaedhil with the Gaill* gives the losses of the Viking-Leinster allies as 2,500 Norsemen and 3,100 Irishmen—5,600 in all. Other accounts give a total of 6,000, or 6,000 foreigners; the highest believable estimate, in the *Leabhar Oiris*, claims 6,700 Viking dead and 1,100 Leinstermen; while several say that the Viking losses numbered not less than 3,000 men, including the 1,000 in mail corselets who had seemingly been commanded by Brodir. In addition, virtually all of their leaders had been killed, including Earl Sigurd, Brodir, Dubhgall and Máelmórdha: it was claimed that no Viking of rank present on the battlefield was left alive at the end of the day. Nevertheless, it was a somewhat Pyrrhic victory—not only was the High King dead, but so too was his son Murchad (he died early the next morning of a mortal wound), his grandson Toirdelbach, who drowned in the pursuit; and his nephew Conaing. At least seven other kings and 1,600 nobles had also been killed. One account puts the losses of the men of Munster and Connacht at 4,000 in all.

Though significant in many respects, the battle of Clontarf was not as decisive as we are often led to believe. It did not mark the end of Scandinavian power in Ireland—that had already begun to wane in the mid-10th century—and King Sigtrygg continued to rule undisturbed in Dublin for another 20 years. However, other than in occasional piratical forays (such as Magnus Barelegs's campaign of 1101), it would be a century and a half before a foreign Scandinavian army again fought on Irish soil.

Hilt of one of some 40 Norwegian and Frankish swords dating from the 9th century, found in the mid-19th century in a large Viking cemetery at Kilmainham, Islandbridge, on the outskirts of Dublin. The patterning on the hilt and pommel is of silver. Spearheads and shield bosses were also discovered. It was near here that the High King Niall Glundubh was decisively defeated by Sigtrygg, king of Dublin, in 919. (National Museum, Dublin)

The Vikings in the East: the Varangian Guard

Although they had been trading in the eastern Baltic since at least the 7th century, the first eastward Viking raid on record took place at the relatively late date of 852, when a Swedish host descended on the city of Novgorod and exacted a huge 'Danegeld' from its citizens. Even thereafter Vikings in the East—always mainly Swedes—tended to be settlers and traders rather than pirates; they were nevertheless quick to establish themselves as rulers over the native Slavic population, who called them *Rus* (whence 'Russia'). By 858 they had established themselves in Kiev, from where, just two years later, they launched a daring—albeit unsuccessful—attack on Constantinople (*Miklagard*, 'The Great Town', as they called it) by sailing their ships down the Dnieper and across the Black Sea. Further major campaigns against the

Front and back views of one of the 64 Gokstad shields (*c*.900), nearly a metre in diameter. The curved metal strengthener and three wooden ribs on the back are modern. The shields of the Gokstad ship were originally painted either black or yellow, and bound round the rim in leather. (Universitetets Oldsaksamling, Oslo)

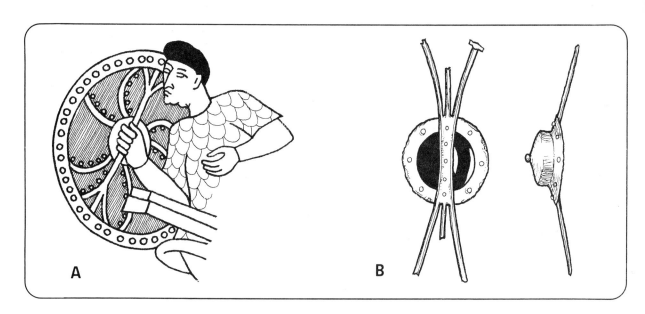

A   **B**

The 10th-century Frostathinglaw and Gulathinglaw required that 'three iron bands' be 'laid across' shields, and that the hand-grip should be fastened on the inside by iron nails. This arrangement doubtless resembled that to be seen in 9th-century Carolingian manuscript illustrations, as depicted in A (where additional, curved strengtheners are also evident). Detail B is an actual excavated example, from a Frankish site. The curved strengtheners of A can also be seen on shields depicted on the Gotland picture stones.

Byzantine Empire were to follow in 907, 941 and 944, by which time the *Rus* had already begun to be assimilated by their Slavic subjects and can no longer truly be regarded as Vikings; indeed, even in the mid-9th century the Arabic geographer Ibn Khordadbah described the *Rus* as a 'kind of Slav'.

Real Vikings, referred to by the *Rus*, Arabs and Byzantines alike as 'Varangians', nevertheless continued to feature in Russian history, sizeable bands of them being hired as mercenaries by successive Kievan and Novgorodian princes—a practice that continued well into the 11th century, the last reference to Viking mercenaries in Russia dating to 1043. Many such Vikings, after a spell in Russia, went on to Constantinople and joined the Byzantine army, in which 700 of them are recorded as early as 911. Thereafter, references to Vikings in Byzantine employ are frequent: seven ships crewed by 415 Vikings from Russia accompanied a Byzantine expedition to Italy in 935; six ships and 629 men sailed on a similar expedition to Crete in 949; *Rus* or Viking troops are recorded fighting the Arabs in 955, and taking part in a campaign in Sicily in 968. Twenty years later, in 988, Vladimir of Kiev sent as many as 6,000 Vikings to the

assistance of Emperor Basil II, and it was from among these that the celebrated Varangian Guard was subsequently established.

The foundation of the Varangian Guard—or the 'Axe-bearing Guard' as it was often termed in Byzantine sources—resulted from Basil II's distrust of his native Byzantine guardsmen. His contrasting confidence in Vladimir's Russian Vikings probably resulted from familiarity with the descriptions of Arab travellers, who recorded how the loyalty of these *Rus* to their own king was such that they were prepared to 'die with him and let themselves be killed for him'. This confidence was not misplaced, since Anna Comnena would later write of 11th century Varangian Guardsmen that 'they regard loyalty to the Emperors and the protection of their persons as a family tradition, a kind of sacred trust and inheritance handed down from generation to generation; this allegiance they preserve inviolate and will never brook the slightest hint of betrayal.' Scandinavians—whether from Sweden, Norway, Denmark or Iceland—were therefore always welcome at the Byzantine court, and the Icelandic sagas and surviving runic inscriptions alike contain innumerable references to men who at one time or another served in the Varangian Guard. Even Harald Hardrada, future king of Norway, became an officer in the Guard.

The Varangian Guard continued to be composed principally of Scandinavians for about a century and a half after its foundation; but after the Norman Conquest of England in 1066 a great many

Norwegian decorated spear sockets. The 'winged' one at the bottom is probably a Frankish import, though the inlay has undoubtedly been added by a Viking craftsman. (Universitetets Oldsaksamling, Oslo)

Anglo-Saxon émigrés also began to be incorporated into its ranks. First recorded in Byzantine employ in the 1070s and 1080s, when they were seemingly brigaded separately from the Scandinavians, these English guardsmen steadily increased in numbers during the 12th century until, by c.1180, the Byzantine chronicler Cinnamus was able to state quite specifically that the Varangian Guard was composed of men 'of British race'. Even so, *Sverrir's Saga* records that as late as 1195 the Emperor despatched envoys to the kings of Norway, Sweden and Denmark requesting 1,200 men for service in the Guard; while Villehardouin's chronicle of the Fourth Crusade of 1202–1204 repeatedly refers to Danish as well as English guardsmen. By this late date, however, they were undoubtedly in the minority, and later 13th century sources invariably refer to the Varangians as being *Englinoi* ('Englishmen'). The Viking adventure in the East was over.

The Vikings in England: 11th century

While Viking power had been waning in Ireland and the East, in England it had undergone an unexpected revival following the accession in 978 of the weak and indecisive King Ethelred *Unraed* ('the poorly-counselled'), remembered by posterity as Ethelred the Unready. Piratical raids resumed in 980 and gradually increased in size and severity over the next 30 years, despite the frequent payment of Danegeld in an attempt to buy the raiders off: 10,000 lbs of silver were paid out thus in 991, and 16,000 lbs in 994, thereafter increasing with each renewed demand to as much as 48,000 lbs by 1012. Encouraged by the lure of such massive sums of money, Danish Vikings raided England almost every year between 997–1014; and the country's ill-led military establishment weakened and collapsed beneath the systematic onslaught that was masterminded by King Swein Forkbeard, king of Denmark c.984–1014. Eventually, in 1013, the people of Northumbria and East Anglia acknowledged Swein as their sovereign, thereby establishing a line of Viking kings of England which comprised Swein (1013–1014); his son Cnut (1016–1035); and the latter's own sons Harald Harefoot (1035–1040) and Harthacnut (1040–1042). Though this line died out with Harthacnut, its claim to the English throne was

This is the celebrated Piraeus Lion, a 12 ft-tall white marble statue which used to stand in the Greek harbour of Piraeus near Athens. Upon its shoulders are the weathered and vandalised remains of two now illegible runic inscriptions relating to Vikings in the service of the Byzantine Emperor (below). Some have tried to find in them references to Harald Hardrada; but the style of the inscriptions is clearly Swedish rather than Norwegian, and they probably date to c.1000 and the second half of the 11th century.

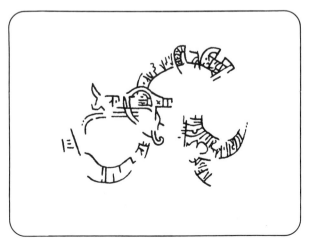

απ ατο ατ ουφ δε τω ρ βατ λει ουρ και τη ρων του γαμετη ρ σ υψ τοιο πα ταρο πε κνοιο αυτη σ · ταβλαπι

Though depicting an event of the 9th century, the artist of the Byzantine *Madrid Skylitzes* portrayed the Emperor's bodyguards as 12th-century Varangian Guardsmen. Eighteen of their famous axes are in evidence, as well as four unit standards and seven spears. (Biblioteca Nacional, Madrid)

later revived by the Norwegian king Harald Sigurdsson, who had inherited it from his nephew Magnus the Good, king of Denmark and Norway 1042–1047.

Harald Sigurdsson, posthumously nicknamed *Hardradi* ('the Ruthless'), had led a checkered and varied career typical of many Viking chieftains. The son of a petty Norwegian king ruling the Ringerike district, he had fought in support of his half-brother King Olaf Haraldsson (St Olaf) at the Battle of Stiklestad in 1030, where the latter was killed. He thereafter fled east to the court of King Jaroslav of Russia. After staying there for several years, during which time he fought against the Poles, he set off to Constantinople 'with a large following' and was enrolled into the celebrated Varangian Guard. He fought against the Arabs in Anatolia and Sicily under Georgios Maniakes, and under other Byzantine generals in southern Italy and Bulgaria, before being imprisoned in Constantinople for apparent misappropriation of Imperial booty taken in the course of these

expeditions. He appears to have escaped during a popular rising against the Emperor Michael Calaphates in 1042, and thereafter returned to Scandinavia via Russia. Reaching Denmark, he assisted Svein Ulfsson in his struggle against Harald's nephew, King Magnus, for the succession to the Danish throne; but went over to Magnus in 1045 in exchange for a half-share in the kingdom of Norway, succeeding to the other half on Magnus's death in 1047.

He was 51 years old when, in 1066, Tostig, the exiled earl of Northumbria and brother of King Harold Godwinsson of England, arrived in Norway in search of military support to regain his lost earldom. Hardrada had had designs on the English throne at least since the 1050s, and needed little encouragement from Tostig. *King Harald's Saga* says that 'the earl and the king talked together often and

A mid-11th-century runic inscription from Ed, Kyrkstigan, Uppland commemorating a Swede who served in the Varangian Guard. It reads: 'Rognvald had these runes carved: in Greece he was leader of the *lith* [war-troop].'

at length; and finally they came to the decision to invade England that summer'. A massive fleet was assembled in the south of Norway: the saga puts it at 240 ships ('apart from supply-ships and smaller craft'); and the *Anglo-Saxon Chronicle* puts it at 300, carrying 'a great pirate host' that has been estimated by modern authorities as numbering at least 9,000–10,000 men, and possibly as many as 18,000. This fleet was joined off the Orkneys by Earl Tostig with 12 vessels of his own, crewed by his household troops and Flemish pirates; from there the whole allied host sailed down to the Humber estuary, plundering as it went, and then upriver as far as Riccall, about ten miles south of York. Here the Norsemen disembarked to confront the Saxon army that had marched against them from York under the command of Earl Morkere of Northumbria and Earl Edwin of Mercia.

'King Harald went ashore and drew up his army,' says *King Harald's Saga*. 'One flank reached down to the river and the other stretched inland along the line of a ditch, where there was a deep and broad morass, full of water. The earls led their army slowly down along the river in close formation. King Harald's banner was near the river, where his line was thickest, but the thinnest part was along the line of the ditch, where his least reliable men were placed. When the earls advanced along the ditch the Norsemen there gave way and the English

followed with Morkere's banner in the van, thinking that the Norsemen would flee.

'When King Harald saw that the English array was advancing down the ditch and was opposite him, he ordered the attack to be sounded and urged his men forward. Ordering his banner Landwaster to be carried in front of him, he made such a severe onslaught that everything gave way before him; and there was a great loss among the men of the earls, and they soon broke in flight, some fleeing upriver and others downriver, but most fled into the marsh, which became so filled up with their dead that the Norsemen could pursue them dry-shod.'

So ended the Battle of Fulford, fought on Wednesday 20 September. The longest version of the *Anglo-Saxon Chronicle* contains only a brief mention of this engagement, claiming that after the earls' army had 'made great slaughter' of the Vikings, 'a great number of the English were either slain or drowned and dispersed in flight, and the Norsemen had possession of the place of slaughter'.

York offered no further resistance to the Vikings, but opened negotiations with Harald, agreeing to accept him as king and to hand over hostages. It was in order to accept these hostages that Harald

The Borrestad memorial stone at Yttergärde, Uppland, Sweden with runic inscription in the form of the Midgard Serpent, recording three expeditions to England in the early 11th century by a man named Ulf. The inscription reads: 'Karsi and Gerbjorn had this stone raised in memory of Ulf their father. God and God's Mother help his soul. And Ulf received Danegeld thrice in England. The first was that which Tosti paid. Then Thorkel [the Tall] paid. Then Cnut paid.' The date of Tosti's Danegeld payment is unknown, but Thorkel and Cnut paid theirs in 1012 and 1016 respectively. (Antikvarisk-Topografiska Arkivet, Stockholm)

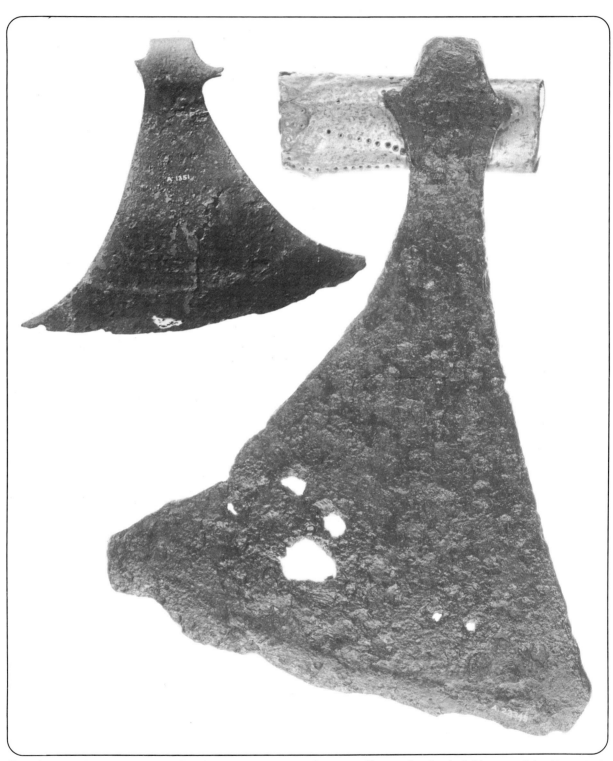

Two of seven 11th-century axeheads found in the Thames near the north side of Old London Bridge. These quite probably date to Olaf Tryggvasson's attack on the Danish-held bridge in 1014 in support of King Ethelred, as is graphically recorded in *Saint Olaf's Saga*, when many Danes were drowned, and some Norwegian ships possibly sank on the site. Olaf's ships 'rowed up under the bridge, laid their cables round the piles which supported it, and then rowed off with their ships as hard as they could downstream. The piles were thus shaken at the bottom and loosened under the bridge . . . and the piles under it being loosened and broken, the bridge gave way; a great part of the men upon it fell into the river, and all the others fled.' It was the poem written by a contemporary Viking skald to commemorate this event that was to evolve over the centuries into the well-known nursery rhyme 'London Bridge Is Falling Down', which assumed its present form in the mid-17th century. (The Museum of London)

encamped at Stamford Bridge, seven miles east of York, on 24 September, having left as much as a third of his army with the fleet at Riccall under the command of Eystein Orri, 'the noblest of all the lendermen [landed men, i.e. nobles]'. The rest of the army was ill-equipped for what was to follow. *King Harald's Saga* describes how, because the weather was hot and sunny, 'they left their armour behind and went ashore with only their shields, helmets and spears, and girt with swords. A number also had bows and arrows, and all were very carefree.' It must therefore have come as a terrible shock to see not hostages approaching the next day, but 'a large force coming towards them. They could see a cloud of dust raised as from horses' hooves, and under it the gleam of handsome shields and white coats-of-mail.' It was another Saxon army, this time led by King Harold Godwinsson himself, and including in its ranks the famed English Huscarls, each of whom one of Hardrada's own marshals had described as 'worth any two of the best men in King Harald's army'. The saga would have it that, in one last attempt to save his errant brother, Harold called for a parley and offered Tostig a third of his kingdom if he would only join him. It was Tostig's enquiry as to what compensation Hardrada would then receive for his trouble that prompted the now-famous reply, 'Seven feet of English soil, or as much more as he is taller than other men.'

Snorri Sturlusson's description of the ensuing battle in *King Harald's Saga*, the only detailed one we have, is suspect on several counts, not least of which is that he appears to have confused aspects of it with the Battle of Hastings. However, it seems likely that when the English army appeared the Norwegians were probably scattered on both sides of the River Derwent, which explains the celebrated incident recorded in the *Anglo-Saxon Chronicle* where 'one Norwegian stood firm against the [advancing] English forces, so that they could not cross the bridge nor clinch victory. An Englishman shot at him with an arrow but to no avail, and another went under the bridge and stabbed him [through a gap in it] under his mail corselet.' This delay, however, had enabled the outnumbered Norsemen to draw up their main body on the further bank, arranging it in a circle bristling with spears and 'with shields overlapping in front and above', against which array the English army now hurled

itself. The saga says that Hardrada 'fell into such a battle-fury that he rushed ahead of his men, fighting two-handed so that neither helmets nor mail corselets could withstand him, and all those who stood in his path gave way. It looked then as if the English were on the point of breaking in flight. . . . But now King Harald was struck in the throat by an arrow, and that was his death-wound. He fell, as did all those who had advanced with him, except for those who retreated with the king's banner.' Earl Tostig then took command, and when the surviving Norsemen were offered quarter by Harold Godwinsson they called back that they would rather die. This, Tostig and most of the remaining Norsemen did.

'At this point', continues the saga, 'Eystein Orri arrived from the ships with all the men he had, who were wearing armour. Eystein got King Harald's banner Landwaster and the fighting began for a third time, even more fiercely than before. The English fell in great numbers and were again on the point of breaking in flight. This stage of the battle was called Orri's Storm. Eystein and his men had run all the way from the ships [where they had received news of the battle from mounted messengers despatched by Hardrada], so fast that they were exhausted and almost unable to fight by the time they arrived; but then they fell into such a battle-fury that they did not even bother to protect themselves with their shields as long as they could still stand. At length they even threw off their mail corselets, and after that it was easy for the English to land blows on them; but others fell and died of exhaustion without so much as a wound on them. Nearly all the leading Norwegians were killed there.

'This happened in the late afternoon. As was to be expected, not everyone reacted in the same way; some fled, and others were lucky enough to escape in various ways. Darkness had fallen before the carnage finally came to an end.' The *Anglo-Saxon Chronicle* says that the Norsemen were pursued all the way back to their ships at Riccall, and that there were few survivors. These were allowed to sail for home in just 24 ships, leaving the flower of Norwegian manhood stretched dead behind them.

Although occasional raids on England continued to be recorded until as late as 1151, and Scandinavian pirates from the Orkneys and the Western Isles were still active even later, it is readily

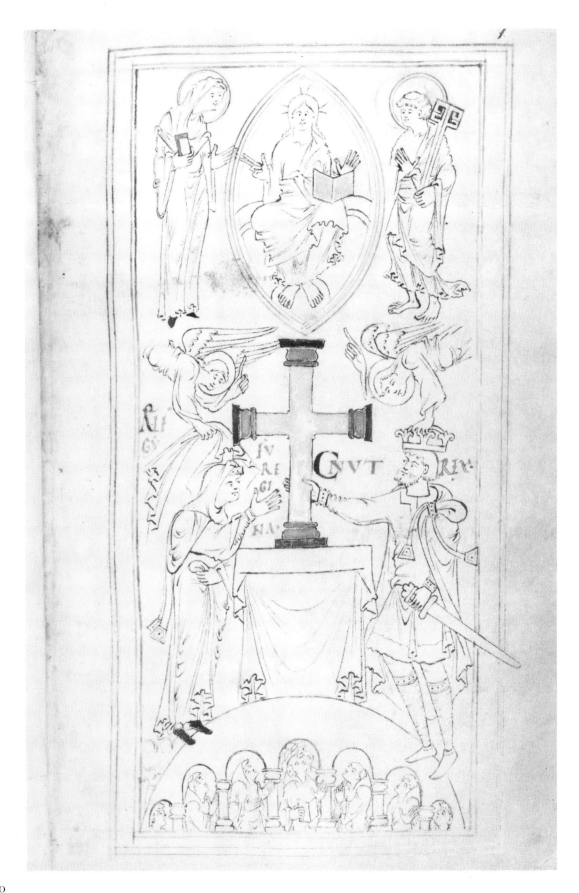

30

apparent why 1066 is generally taken to mark the end of the Viking era, and why Harald Hardrada is often dubbed 'the last Viking'. His was the last great enterprise of the Viking age. Night was now falling on the long Viking day that had begun nearly 300 years earlier.

Viking Warfare

Tactics

When fighting amongst themselves, the Vikings' major battles almost invariably took place at sea—witness Hafrs Fjord in 872, Svöldr in 1000 and Nissa in 1062, to cite but three examples. Nevertheless, they made every effort to ensure that a naval action was as much like a land battle as possible, arranging their fleets in lines or wedges; one side—or sometimes both—customarily roped together the largest of their ships gunwale to gunwale to form large, floating platforms. The biggest and best-manned ships usually formed the middle part of the line, with the commander's vessel invariably positioned in the very centre, since he normally had the largest vessel of all. High-sided merchantmen were sometimes positioned on the flanks of the line too. The prows of the longer ships extended out in front of the battle-line and some of them, called *bardi*, were therefore armoured with iron plates at stem and stern, which bore the brunt of the fighting. Some even had a series of iron spikes called a beard (*skegg*) round the prow, designed to hole enemy ships venturing close enough to board.

In addition to this floating platform there were usually a number of additional individual ships positioned on the flanks and in the rear, whose tasks were to skirmish with their opposite numbers; to attack the enemy platform if he had one; to put reinforcements aboard their own platform when necessary; and to pursue the enemy in flight. Masts were lowered in battle, and all movement was by oar, so the loss of a ship's oars in collision with another vessel effectively crippled it. Nevertheless, the classical *diekplus* manoeuvre, which involved shearing off an enemy vessel's oars with the prow of

one's own ship, does not seem to have been deliberately employed, and nor was ramming.

The main naval tactic was simply to row against an enemy ship, grapple and board it, and clear it with hand weapons before moving on to another vessel, sometimes cutting the cleared ship loose if it formed the wing of a platform. The platforms were attacked by as many ships as could pull alongside. Boarding was usually preceded by a shower of arrows and, at closer range, javelins, iron-shod stakes and stones, as a result of which each oarsman was often protected by a second man, who deflected missiles with his shield. On the final approach prior to boarding, shields were held overhead 'so closely that no part of their holders was left uncovered'. Some ships carried extra supplies of stones and other missiles. Stones are extensively recorded in accounts of Viking naval battles, and were clearly the favourite form of missile. The largest were dropped from high-sided vessels on to (and even through) the decks of ships which drew alongside to board.

When raiding, the Vikings preferred to beach their ships on a small island or eyot, or in the curve of a river, throwing up a rampart and stockade on any side which could be approached by land. The resultant fortified encampment was usually left with a garrison, since the Vikings took care to protect their lines of communication: failure to do so could result in utter rout and heavy losses. These camps might also be used as a refuge in face of a superior enemy force: they were rarely attacked successfully, the besiegers tending to disperse after a period of inactivity.

In land-battles the Vikings' favoured battle-formation was a shield-wall—a massive phalanx of men several ranks deep (apparently five or more) with the better-armed and armoured men forming the front ranks. On occasion they might form up in two or even more such shield-walls, as they did at the battles of Ashdown and Meretun in 871, and at Corbridge in 918 (where one of the four divisions they formed was held in reserve in a concealed position). There is some debate as to just how close-packed the shield-wall formation actually was. Contemporary literary references indicate that hand-to-hand combat involved a considerable degree of violent movement, and the amount of twisting, dodging and leaping back and forth that this entailed makes it seem improbable that the men's shields overlapped. Nevertheless, a 10th-century hogback tombstone in Gosforth, Cumbria, carries a relief of a shield-wall in which the shields are overlapped up to about half their width (which would give a frontage of only about 18 ins per man) and the 9th-century Oseberg tapestry similarly includes a shield-wall of partially overlapping shields. Snorri Sturlusson too, in his description of the Battle of Stamford Bridge in *King Harald's Saga*, tells us that the Norsemen there drew up with their shields 'overlapping in front and above'. Interestingly, members of a present-day re-enactment organisation, the Norse Film and Pageant Society, who use reproductions of Viking weapons and armour, have made the observation that in close combat any extra elbow-room required for a good swing with an axe or sword was best found by pushing into the enemy formation rather than by standing in line in one's own ranks. This would tend to support the hypothesis that shields were probably initially interlocked, to receive the impact of the first enemy charge, but that thereafter the shield-wall tended to loosen up automatically.

The Vikings' main variation on the simple phalanx was the *svynfylking* or 'swine-array', a wedge-shaped formation said to have been originated by Odin himself, which testifies to its antiquity. Described in *Flateyjarbok* as having two men in the first rank, three in the second and five in the third, it could be fielded either singly or in multiples joined at the base, the whole line thus resembling a zig-zag. If Snorri can be trusted, the shield-wall could also be drawn up as a circular formation, since he describes Harald Hardrada's army at Stamford Bridge as arrayed in 'a long and rather thin line, with the wings bent back until they met, thus forming a wide circle of even depth all the way round'. Snorri also says that on this occasion the archers remained in the open centre of the circular shield-wall; normally they drew up to the rear with the other missile-men—spear-throwers, stone-throwers and the like—and fired overhead. Commanders were protected by a separate shield-wall of bodyguards whose job was to deflect missiles.

The Vikings were usually uncomfortable fighting against cavalry, though generally they seem to have succeeded in retiring in good order, and were even capable of rallying and winning the day. The Battle of Saucourt in 881, where they are recorded to have lost as many as 8,000–9,000 men, was their first decisive defeat at the hands of Frankish cavalry (who were the best in Western Europe at that date), and even that was a close-run thing. When their first attack had seemed successful, the Franks had made the tactical error of breaking ranks in order to start looting, upon which a Viking counter-attack nearly broke them. A second charge by the Franks forced the Vikings to withdraw, once again in good order despite their incredibly heavy losses. In the East, too, they are recorded as being at a disadvantage when confronted by cavalry, as in the fighting with the Byzantines around Silistria in 972. A rare instance of Vikings facing feudal cavalry is recorded in *Heimskringla*, when in 1151 in Northern England, a raiding party defeated mounted knights and supporting infantry by their use of archery.

Despite the fact that they fought mostly on foot the Vikings also occasionally fielded cavalry, as at the Battle of Sulcoit in Ireland in 968; and at the Battle of Montfaucon in France in 888, at which the chronicler Abbo of Fleury implies a large body of Viking cavalry was present, fighting separately from their infantry. More usually, however, they used horses simply as a means of increasing their mobility during their raiding expeditions. They either rounded up horses for this purpose in the vicinity of their encampment, or took those of the defeated enemy after a battle, as is recorded in the *Anglo-Saxon Chronicle* under the years 999 and 1010. No doubt the horses they brought with them to England from France in 885 and 892 had been similarly captured from defeated Frankish armies.

One last feature of Scandinavian warfare still in evidence in the Viking era was the 'hazelled field'. This was a specially chosen battlefield, fenced with hazel branches on all sides, where a battle was fought at a prearranged time and date by mutual agreement of the protagonists. Once challenged to fight in a hazelled field it was apparently a dishonour to refuse, or to ravage your opponent's territory until after the battle had been fought. The English were not unaware of this somewhat archaic tradition, since according to *Egil's Saga* the Battle of Vinheidr, identified with the Battle of Brunanburh in 937, took place in just such a hazelled field, which had been prepared by King Athelstan in order to delay the Vikings and their assorted Welsh and Scottish allies from pillaging until he had been able

Viking warriors, 9th-10th centuries; see Plates commentaries for all details of this and other colour illustrations.

A

B

Viking warriors, 9th–10th centuries

1   2   3

C

Viking women, 9th-10th centuries

1   2   3

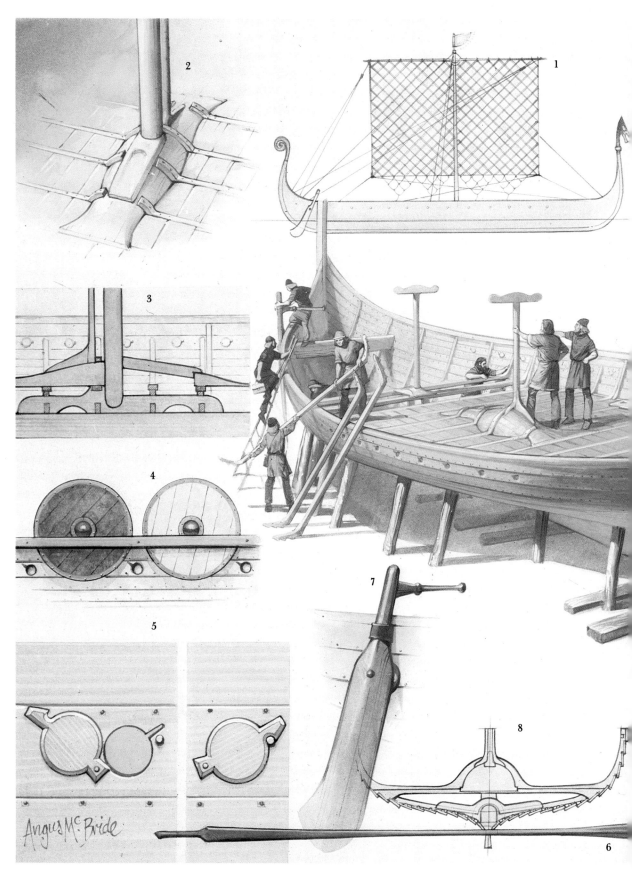

2

1

3

4

5

7

8

6

Angus McBride

D

Viking ship construction

E

A sea-battle, based on 'King Olaf Tryggvasson's Saga'

A strandhögg

F

Eastern Vikings, 10th-11th centuries

G

Trelleborg military camp, Denmark

H

Battle between Vikings and 'Skraelings', 11th century

I

Viking warriors, 12th century

J

to assemble a large enough army to defeat them. The latest reference to such a hazelled field that I am aware of dates to 978, when Earl Hakon Sigurdsson of Norway defeated King Ragnfrid (one of Eric Bloodaxe's sons) in a field marked out with *hoslur*.

The Jomsvikings

One by-product of the Viking age had been the establishment of independent military brotherhoods or guilds known as Viking-unions or Viking-laws (*Vikinge-lag*), which comprised bodies of warriors—effectively mercenary 'Free Companies' —living together under their own strict codes of conduct. They did not seek to conquer land on their own behalf, but every summer were prepared to hire themselves out to kings and princes in exchange for pay.

The most famous (and most hotly-debated) such brotherhood was that of the *Jomsvikingelag*, or Jomsvikings, which, though it does not feature in any surviving contemporary source, was later the subject of its own Icelandic saga. According to later Danish accounts the Jomsvikings were established in Wendland in the late 10th century (probably the 980s) by King Harald Bluetooth of Denmark, banished from his own kingdom by his son Swein Forkbeard. The fortress of Jomsborg, which he reputedly founded, was probably at or near Wollin, Adam of Bremen's *Jumne*, at the mouth of the Oder. It had an artificial harbour, its entrance guarded by a tower over a stone archway with iron gates, reported in the oldest extant manuscript as being capable of holding three ships—a figure later increased to 300 or 360. One version says that Harald taught the Wends piracy, and Jomsborg itself may in fact have been garrisoned by Wends commanded by Danes; certainly at the Battle of Svöldr one of the 11 Jomsviking ships present was crewed by Wends. *Jomsviking Saga*, however, would have it that Jomsborg was a purely Viking stronghold established by Swein Forkbeard's foster-father, Pálnatóki. Either way, most accounts seem to agree that the leader of the Jomsvikings in their heyday at the end of the 10th century was Earl Sigvald, son of a petty king named Strut-Harald who had ruled over Scania in Sweden (at this time counted as part of Denmark).

If the saga is to be believed, the rules by which the Jomsvikings lived were extremely strict. Membership of their brotherhood was restricted to men of outstanding strength, aged between 18 and 50, who were obliged to live peaceably together and 'to kindle no slander against one another'. They were never to show any sign of fear, 'however hopeless matters looked', and flight in the face of an enemy of equal strength was forbidden. Their commander was to have judgement over blood-feuds, but each Jomsviking was expected to avenge his comrades-in-arms as if they were his own brothers. All booty was to be handed in for equal distribution amongst the guild members. No-one was to be absent for more than three days without permission, no women were to be admitted to the fortress, and neither women nor children were to be taken captive. Anyone breaking these rules was to be ejected from the brotherhood immediately.

14th-century illustration depicting the death of King Olaf Haraldsson (St Olaf) at the Battle of Stiklestad in 1030. *Saint Olaf's Saga* **describes the event thus: 'Thorstein Knaresmed struck at King Olaf with his axe and hit his left leg above the knee.... Then Thore Hund struck at him with his spear, and the stroke went in under his ring-shirt and into his belly. Then Kalf struck at him on the left side of the neck.... These three wounds were the death of King Olaf, and after his death the greater part of the forces which had advanced with him fell with him.'**

Mail corselets from Vaerdalen, North Trondelag and Romul, Melhus, South Trondelag. Archaeological and saga evidence indicates that those worn in the 8th–11th centuries were identical. (Universitetets Oldsaksamling, Oslo)

'Every summer they went out and made war in different countries, got high renown, and were looked on as the greatest of warriors; hardly any others were thought their equals at this time.' So says the *Jomsviking Saga*, while *King Olaf Tryggvasson's Saga* observes that 'at that time it was considered prestigious to have Jomsborg Vikings with an army'. The truth of the matter would appear to be somewhat different, however, since all three of the major campaigns in which the sources claim the brotherhood participated ended in disaster for their employers: Styrbjorn Starki, contending for the throne of Sweden, was beaten by his uncle, Eric the Victorious at Fyrisvold near Uppsala; Swein Forkbeard's attack on Earl Hakon of Norway was disastrously defeated at Hjörungavag *c*.990; and King Olaf Tryggvasson of Norway was defeated and killed by the Swedes and Danes at Svöldr in 1000. All three defeats appear to have resulted from the same cause—that Earl Sigvald had a nasty tendency to cut and run if the prospects began to look dubious! This is probably why *King Olaf Tryggvasson's Saga* describes him as 'a prudent, ready-minded man'.

King Magnus the Good of Norway destroyed Jomsborg in 1043, 'killing many people, burning and destroying both in the town and in the country all around, and wreaking the greatest havoc'. However, the nucleus of the Jomsvikings guild appears to have disbanded much earlier, probably after Earl Sigvald's death some time before 1010. Remnants of the Jomsvikings are said to have accompanied Earl Sigvald's brothers Heming and Thorkel the Tall to England in 1009, where in time they may have become the nucleus of King Cnut's *Tinglith*, the royal bodyguard that was to evolve into the celebrated Huscarls.

Berserks and Wolfcoats

In the pagan era, before Scandinavia was converted to Christianity, the *berserkir* were looked upon as possessing supernatural powers attributed to the Vikings' chief god, Odin. *Ynglinga Saga* records how in battle they 'rushed forward without armour, were as mad as dogs or wolves, bit their shields and were as strong as bears or wild boars, and killed people at a single blow, while neither fire nor iron could hurt them. This was called the berserk fury.' Today, we still refer to someone in a mad rage as

having 'gone berserk'.

In reality this berserk fury was probably a form of paranoia, possibly related to a belief in lycanthropy, while in some cases it may even have been prompted by an epileptic attack. Whatever it was, it was clearly an hereditary condition rather than something that could be learnt. One account actually tells us that a particular man's 12 sons were all berserks: 'It was their custom, if they were with their own men when they felt the berserk fury coming on, to go ashore and wrestle with large stones or trees; otherwise in their rage they would have slain their friends.'

Evidence for belief in lycanthropy can be found in *Volsunga Saga*, wherein we are told that Sigmund and his son Sinfjotli donned wolfskins, used the speech of wolves and howled when attacked; and in the legend of Hrolf Kraki, whose berserk champion, Bothvar Bjarki, reputedly fought in the likeness of a huge bear. Certainly wolves and bears are the animals most frequently associated with berserks, for whom an alternative name was in fact *ulfhednar* ('wolfcoats' or 'wolfskin-clad ones'). This would seem to confirm beyond reasonable doubt that *berserkir* originally meant 'bear-shirt', and not 'bare-shirt' as has so often been suggested.

The *Hrafnsmal* describes berserks as men of great valour who never flinched in battle. This, along with the special favour with which Odin clearly regarded them, meant that they were to be found among the bodyguards of most pagan Viking kings, a troop of 12 being most commonly encountered in the sources. They fought in the forefront of every land-battle and from the forecastle of the king's ship at sea. *Harald Fairhair's Saga* relates how on his ship 'the forecastle men were picked men for they had the king's banner. From the stem to the mid-hold was called the *rausn*, or the fore-defence; and there the berserks were to be found. Such men only were received into King Harald's house-troop as were remarkable for strength, courage, and all kinds of dexterity; and they alone got a place in his ship.' It was probably berserks to whom Snorri Sturlusson was referring in his description of the Battle of Svöldr in 1000, where some men on King Olaf's ship forgot they were not fighting on land and 'rushed madly at the enemy, fell overboard and were drowned'.

In later, Christian Iceland the berserk fury was

48

actually outlawed, and berserks were regarded as some sort of ungodly fiend, whom the sagas represented as mindless bullies fit only to be cut down by an appropriate hero. It is possible that this attitude was also adopted in Christian Scandinavia.

The Raven standard

From the outset Viking armies had probably been accompanied by war-flags (*gunnefanes*) bearing devices such as fanged, winged monsters: so at least we may suppose from the *Fulda Annals'* description of their standards as *signia horribilia*; and we know that even the Christian king Olaf Tryggvasson had a white standard bearing a serpent. However, the most widely-recorded Viking standards were those bearing raven devices. Cnut, for instance, had a raven-embroidered white silk flag at the Battle of Ashingdon in 1016, while the *Anglo-Saxon Chronicle* records the capture of a standard actually called *Reafan* ('Raven') as early as 878. According to the *Annals of St Neots*, if 'Reafan' fluttered it signified a Viking victory, but if it drooped it meant a defeat.

Similar magical properties were attributed to the raven standard of Earl Sigurd of Orkney. It had been made for him by his mother, who was reputedly a sorceress, and is described as 'very cleverly embroidered in the shape of a raven, and when the banner fluttered in the breeze it seemed as if the raven spread its wings'. According to *Orkneyinga Saga* Sigurd's mother gave it to him with the warning that 'it will bring victory to the man it's carried before, but death to the one who carries it'. Sure enough, in the very first engagement in which it was carried Sigurd's standard-bearer was killed as soon as battle commenced: 'The earl told another man to pick up the banner but before long he was killed too. The earl lost three standard-bearers, but he won the battle.'

Some years later the same standard actually accompanied Earl Sigurd at the Battle of Clontarf. *Njal's Saga* records how Kerthjalfad, a foster-son of the Irish High King Brian Boru, 'burst through Earl Sigurd's ranks right up to the banner, and killed the standard-bearer. The earl ordered someone else to carry the standard, and the fighting flared up again. Kerthjalfad at once killed the new standard-

Saxon Huscarls, from the Bayeux Tapestry. Forming the nucleus of the Late Saxon army, the Huscarls had in fact been introduced into England as a sort of royal bodyguard either by Swein Forkbeard or under his son Cnut. At first they numbered either 3,000 or 6,000 men, probably the former, and were constantly in attendance on the king; but by 1066 some were being granted gifts of land on which to settle, while others were deployed as garrison troops to places of strategic importance.

bearer and all those who were near him. Earl Sigurd ordered Thorstein Hallsson to carry the standard, and Thorstein was about to take it when Amundi the White said, "Don't take the banner, Thorstein. All those who bear it get killed." "Hrafn the Red," said the earl, "you take the standard." "Carry your own devil yourself," said Hrafn. The earl then said, "A beggar should carry his own bundle", and he ripped the flag from its staff and tucked it under his clothing. A little later Amundi the White was killed, and then the earl himself died with a spear through him.'

In the same way that Sigurd's raven standard was woven by his mother, the 'Reafan' standard captured by the Saxons in 878 is recorded to have been woven for the Danish commander there —a son of Ragnar Lodbrok (probably Ubbi)— by his own sisters. The undisguised implication was that they too must have been sorceresses, responsible for imbuing it with its victory-bringing powers. Indeed, the ability of a raven standard to impart victory was deep-rooted in pagan Scandinavian religion, since the raven was the bird of Odin, the god of war, and was associated with battlefield

11th-century carved head in elk-horn, wearing a decorated conical helmet with nasal, from Sigtuna, Uppland, Sweden. (Antikvarisk-Topografiska Arkivet, Stockholm)

slaughter throughout the Germanic world. It therefore seems likely that Harald Hardrada's flag *Landeythan* ('Landwaster') similarly bore a raven, since it 'was said to bring victory to the man before whom it was borne in battle—and that had been so ever since he got it'. Even as late as King Sverri of Norway's reign (1184–1202) we read, in *Sverri's Saga*, of a lenderman saying: 'Let us hoist the standard before the king . . . and let us hew a sacrifice beneath the raven's talons.'

The Plates

A & B: *Viking warriors, 9th–10th centuries*
Basic Viking costume comprised a long-sleeved woollen or linen tunic reaching to mid-thigh or just below the knee (often worn over a fine wool or linen shirt), plus trousers which came in an assortment of styles: close-fitting like ski-trousers (A3); untapered (A1); or exceedingly baggy and gathered below the knee (B1). Some were only knee-length, with separate leggings, often cross-gartered from knee to ankle (A2). Stockinged breeches, sometimes of fur or leather, might also be worn. Shoes were of soft leather, sometimes with wooden soles, winter pairs having the fur left on for warmth. Rough cowhide or sealskin boots might also be worn, hairy side out. A short cape or a longer cloak, pinned at the right shoulder, or sometimes at the hip (A4), completed the Vikings' everyday dress. This cloak might be of rich cloth and fur-lined, while some woollen ones, called *roggvarfeldr*, were made to look like shaggy fur by the incorporation of tufts of unspun wool in the weaving: this type of cloak was particularly popular in Iceland and Ireland and became fashionable in Norway under King Harald Greycloak (hence his name).

Popular clothing colours included red, scarlet, reddish-brown, brown, blue, green, white, black and grey: of these red, leaf-green and blue were clearly the favourites. Trousers might be striped vertically—one warrior in *Njal's Saga* wears blue-striped trousers—and one anecdote records that woollen leggings should be brown or any other colour except scarlet. Tunics often had hems and panels of tablet-woven cloth, patterned in coloured silk and metal thread. Similarly woven headbands might also be worn (B3).

Viking men were vain about their appearance and bathed and changed their clothes regularly. They were almost invariably bearded (the beard being looked upon as proof of masculinity), some Vikings wearing their beards forked (A3), or plaited (A1, B1). Hair might likewise be plaited (B3), and was generally worn long enough at least to cover the neck, though it could be considerably longer—that of Brodir of Man is supposed to have been so long that he tucked it into his belt in battle. Hair colouring ranged from blonde and red to black, darker hair generally being more common amongst the Danes.

Basic armament comprised sword or axe, spear, and shield, while most men had a short knife attached to their belts. Of these weapons the sword was clearly the most popular and was treated with a certain amount of reverence, especially in the case of old swords that had been handed down from generation to generation or looted from burial mounds. A certain mystique clung to such weapons, which were usually given high-sounding names such as *Brynjubitr* ('Byrnie-biter'), *Langhvass* ('Long-and-sharp') and *Gullinhjalti* ('Golden-hilted'). The very best swords were imported from the Frankish

kingdoms, though Viking craftsmen usually fitted them with ornate hilts and grips of metal, bone, horn, and walrus ivory. These were often decorated in gold, copper, silver or niello. The grips of simpler swords might be just plain wood, covered in leather. Sword blades, usually pattern-welded and sometimes inlaid, averaged about 32 ins. in length, were two-edged, and had a shallow groove, or 'fuller', on either side to reduce their weight. The single-edged sword, or *sax*, also remained in use at the beginning of the Viking age, particularly in Norway. Scabbards were of wood, covered in tooled leather, with a bronze chape and a rust-repellent lining such as oiled leather, waxed cloth, or sheepskin with the wool left on. It could be either girded or suspended from a baldric which, like the waist-belt, was buckled and often decorated with bronze or silver mounts.

Before the Viking era began the axe had been virtually abandoned in warfare everywhere else in Europe, and its reintroduction in the 9th–11th centuries, especially in England and Ireland, was solely due to the Vikings, amongst whom its popularity had never waned. There were three principal types in use during this period, these being the *skeggox* or 'bearded axe' (in use by the 8th century); an indeterminate type that is usually called simply a 'hand-axe' (A2); and the *breidox* or 'broad-axe' (B2). The last type, with its distinctive crescentic blade, first appeared at the end of the 10th century and is most famous for its use by the Anglo-Danish Huscarls at the Battle of Hastings in 1066. The blade of such an axe, which usually had a welded-on cutting edge of specially hardened iron, could be 12 ins. across according to the chronicler Wace, while *Laxdaela Saga* mentions one that measured 18 ins. along its curved edge. Like the sword, the axe was often given a name, but of a somewhat less reverent nature; Snorri Sturlusson wrote that 'men call axes by the names of she-trolls'. That of St Olaf was named *Hel*, after the Viking goddess of death.

The third of the Vikings' principal weapons was the ash spear (*spjot*), of which both throwing and thrusting types existed. The former had narrow

A selection of the famous 12th-century Scandinavian or Hebridean chessmen found at Uig, on the Isle of Lewis. Three of them are biting the rims of their shields, so are presumably intended to represent berserks. The figure on the extreme right wears a *vida stalhufa* or 'wide steel hat', an early example of a kettle-helmet. (The Trustees of the British Museum)

blades and slim shafts while the latter had broad, leaf-shaped blades and thicker, iron-shod shafts. Blades of both types were ribbed, often decorated, and invariably socketed, some of them with short side-lobes usually referred to as 'wings'. Skill at spear-throwing was greatly admired, and Olaf Tryggvasson was justly famous for his ability to throw a spear from each hand simultaneously.

Shields were circular, constructed of wood, and might be leather-covered. They were bound round the edges with iron, or leather in the Gokstad examples, while one found at Birka in Sweden was

Drawings from contemporary representations of berserks. (A) Taken from the 9th-century Oseberg tapestry, this man appears to be clothed in fur, is armed with shield and spear, and is probably wearing a helmet under his fur hood. (B) This warrior actually predates the Viking era, being taken from a 7th-century helmet plaque which clearly depicts a man dressed in the pelt of a wolf, therefore an *ulfhednar*. The naked warrior alongside him is probably one of Odin's champions, the *einherjar* ('belonging to an army'); horned helmets such as the one depicted were never worn in the Viking era except in pictures of gods and, possibly, pagan priests.

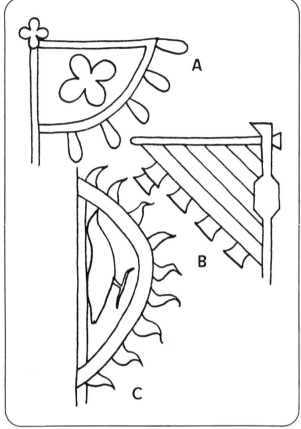

Viking standards. (A) Taken from a silver penny of Olaf Sihtricsson, minted in York *c*.942. (B) Taken from a coin of Cnut's reign. (C) A raven standard from the Bayeux Tapestry; bearing in mind the Normans' fairly recent Viking ancestry, it is not unreasonable to suppose that this raven standard was a treasured heirloom of some Norman family, brought out of safekeeping to accompany William the Conqueror's great enterprise.

bound with small bronze plates. In the centre was a prominent hemispherical or conical iron boss, behind which was the hand-grip (A1). The shield itself was usually between 30 and 40 ins. in diameter and made of limewood, only about one-fifth of an inch thick and consequently very light. If the Gotland picture stones are accurate some shields may have been smaller. They were generally painted, the colours most often referred to in the sources being red (by far the most popular), yellow, black, white, and to a lesser extent green and blue; the 64 shields found with the Gokstad ship were painted alternately in yellow and black. The orb

Viking horseman carved into an 8th-century picture stone at Lillbjärs, Gotland. Note his conical helmet with earguards, also his baggy trousers. The figure beneath the horse's front legs appears to be wearing either mail or a quilted corselet. (Antikvarisk-Topografiska Arkivet, Stockholm)

could also be divided up into halves and quarters painted in contrasting colours, and there are some references to shields painted with mythical scenes, dragons and other creatures. At the Battle of Nesjar in 1015 many of St Olaf's men had gilt, red, or blue crosses on their white shields; this was a nominally Christian Norwegian army, fighting against its own unconverted countrymen. The Gotland picture stones show many shields patterned like that of A3.

Though only a few fragments have actually survived—the most complete example being that from Gjermundbu in Norway (A2)—most Viking warriors appear to have possessed helmets. Most were probably simple conical types with or without a nasal, but some had decorated eyebrow ridges inlaid with copper and silver (A1). In battle they

often had a *herkumbl* ('war-mark') painted on the front, presumably some kind of identifying badge or sign.

Mail corselets, called *brynja* or *hringserkr* ('ring-shirt'), were at first considerably less common than helmets, probably only being worn by the wealthy, and with the exception of a few fragmentary finds no Viking-age corselets have come down to us. One of the most complete examples was again found at Gjermundbu, made of interlocking rings with overlapping, unriveted ends. In the earlier part of this period they were probably short-sleeved and reached to the hips or to just above the knee (A1). By the 11th century they could be somewhat longer, Harald Hardrada's being recorded as so long that it reached nearly to mid-calf, and so strong that no weapon could pierce it. (It was probably its length that gave this corselet its feminine name 'Emma'!)

Reconstruction of the bridle found in the Gokstad ship burial. (Universitetets Oldsaksamling, Oslo)

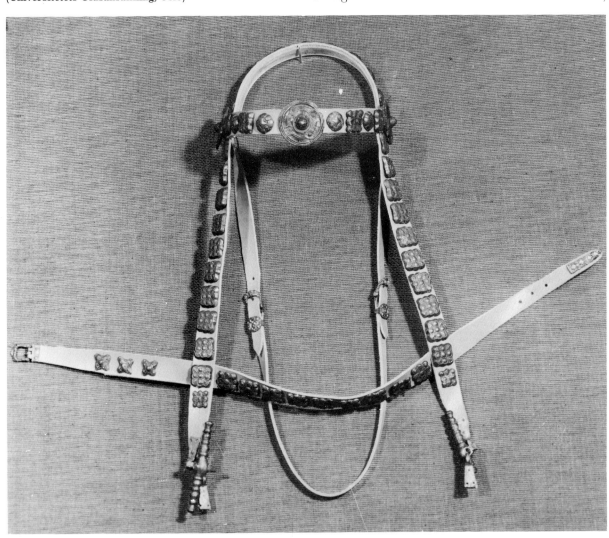

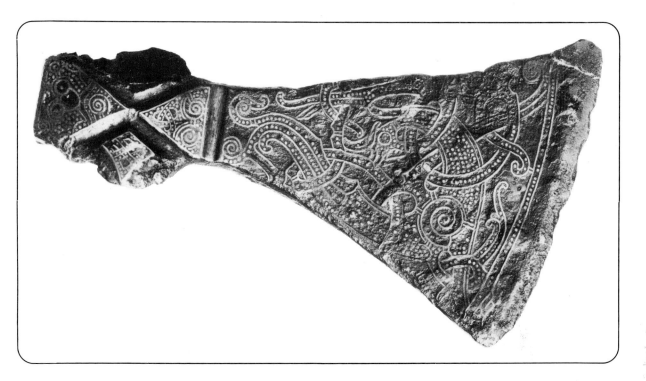

Small axehead, 6.5 ins. long, from Mammen, Jutland; it is inlaid with silver wire decoration in the 'Mammen style', to which it gave its name, and which is characterised by writhing animal ornamentation. (Nationalmuseet, Copenhagen)

It is reasonable to suppose, in fact, that a well-off, fully-equipped Viking warrior of the mid-11th century would have looked little different from the Anglo-Danish Huscarls depicted in the Bayeux Tapestry (B2). Significantly, the sagas tend to indicate that 11th-century Vikings often found these heavier corselets irksome and too hot to wear in battle; Hardrada's Norsemen in 1066, for instance, left their armour behind with the ships prior to Stamford Bridge, and King Magnus the Good 'threw from him his ring-shirt' before joining battle with the Wends at Lyrskog Heath in 1043. Less wealthy warriors substituted padded leather jerkins in place of mail (A3): 12 reindeer-hide corselets were brought from Lapland by Thore Hund in 1029, which 'no weapon could cut or pierce any more than if they had been made of mail, nor even as much'.

Though they favoured hand-weapons the Vikings nevertheless made considerable use of the bow on both land and sea, especially the Norwegians (recorded as 'famous bowmen') and the Swedes (the word 'bow' being sometimes used in Sweden to denote a warrior). Even kings were known to wield bows in battle, taking great pride in their personal accuracy. Surviving fragments indicate that wooden self-bows were used, of which some were of the proportions of medieval longbows—one found in Ireland measures 73 ins. in length and has a D-shaped cross-section. Up to 40 arrows were carried, held in a cylindrical quiver at the waist (B3). The arrowheads were a mixture of tanged and socketed types.

C: Viking women

Though there were doubtless subtle trends in fashion over the years, female attire appears to have remained fundamentally unchanged throughout the Viking age, as is confirmed by the sagas and contemporary pictorial sources such as the Gotland picture stones, small figurines, and the Oseberg tapestry. Basic costume comprised a long woollen or linen chemise, usually pleated, either short-sleeved or sleeveless (women apparently liking to show off their arms), and either sewn or drawn tight by a ribbon at the neck. Over this was worn an outer garment consisting of two lengths of wool or even silk, joined across the shoulders by straps secured with bronze 'tortoise' brooches some four or five inches long. Some authorities have suggested instead that the two pieces of the outer garment may have been wrapped around the body, one from

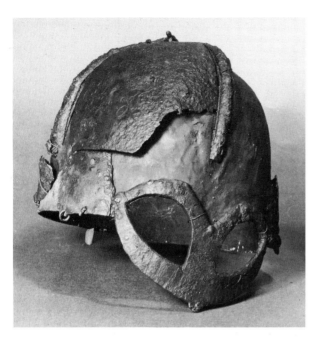

This reconstruction of a 10th-century Viking helmet is based on fragments found in a grave at Gjermundbu, Ringerike, Norway. It has a 'spectacle'-like nose/eye guard, and strengthening bands across the crown. (Universitetets Oldsaksamling, Oslo)

scissors, keys and needle cases—were suspended by cords or fine chains.

The sagas tend to indicate that the majority of Scandinavian women were, unsurprisingly, fair-skinned, blue-eyed and blonde-haired, and another 10th-century Arab, al-Tartusi, adds that they wore attractive eye make-up. Married women wore their hair knotted under a scarf or cap, while maidens wore theirs loose, sometimes with a headband to hold it in place. Most of the contemporary depictions of women show a large knot behind the head which has been variously interpreted as a scarf, ribbon or hair.

D: Details of Viking ship construction

Most Viking ships were built in winter, after the end of the farming year. They were made completely of oak whenever possible, so that today there are very few oak trees to be found anywhere in Scandinavia. As oak became more scarce pine, ash, birch, alder, linden (lime) and willow began to be used for various parts of ships, though the keel remained invariably of oak. Oak was also preferred for the stem and stern, and the kerling (*kjerringa*, or 'old woman')—a timber block on which the base of the mast rested. A long and hard search must have been undertaken to find an oak tree tall enough to provide the keel of the *Long Serpent*, of which the portion that rested on the grass during its construction was 74 Scandinavian 'ells' long (i.e. about 113 ft), excluding stem and stern. The building procedure was for the keel to be laid down first, to which the stem and stern pieces were then fitted. The hull was then constructed from rows of strakes, nailed together overlapping downwards (i.e. clinker-built) and caulked with tarred rope.

On warships the strakes were thin so as to save weight. There was a well-known episode during the construction of the *Long Serpent* in which the shipwright, Thorberg Skafhogg, deliberately hacked chunks out of its planking and then smoothed down the strakes individually to the depth of the notches he had thereby inflicted, 'and the king and all present declared that the ship was much handsomer on the side of the hull which Thorberg had thinned, and bade him shape the other side the same way, and gave him great thanks for the improvement'. The strakes of the Gokstad ship were about an inch thick on the bottom, up to 1.7 ins.

right to left and the other from left to right, though still secured in the same way. The complete absence of belt-buckles in women's graves would indicate that their dresses usually either hung loose, or were tied with a fabric belt. However, at least one saga refers to a dress being taken in at the waist to suit the wearer's figure. Knee-length hose were worn under the chemise, and a heavy cloak and fur hat might be worn in winter.

The large 'tortoise' brooches were at first highly ornate, some being silver-plated or even gilded; but later examples are cruder, probably because by the 9th century a fine woollen shawl was also being worn, which would have covered them. The brooch securing the shawl then became richly decorated instead. A 10th-century Arab traveller, Ibn Fadlan, was of the opinion that the women's 'tortoise' brooches actually indicated the wealth of their husbands, depending on whether they were made of iron, silver, copper or gold. Other jewellery comprised bracelets, rings, necklaces, and festoons between the 'tortoise' brooches; the last two both consisted of beads and pendants of amber or coloured glass (especially green), though some were made of precious metals. From another brooch various implements—such as combs, small knives, thick at the waterline. One of the topmost strakes contained the oar-holes, each with its own little pivoted shutter to prevent water from coming through when the ship was under sail. The ribs were only put into place after the ship had been constructed up to the waterline, the strakes being lashed to them with spruce-roots rather than being nailed on, which gave the hull a considerable degree of flexibility.

D1 shows a reconstruction of the type of rigging that may have been used on Viking ships, complete with what the sagas call a *beiti-ass*: apparently, a diagonal spar which was used to hold a corner of the square sail and thereby enable the ship to sail closer to the wind. The various other details depict the 'mast-fish' (D2 and D3); the steering-oar (D7); the Oseberg ship's shield-rack arrangement (D4); an oar from the Oseberg ship (D6); and the oar-ports of the Gokstad ship, with their individual shutters (D5). D8 is a midship section through the Gokstad ship.

E: A sea-battle

Though naval tactics have already been covered, the following passage from *King Olaf Tryggvasson's Saga* is included in order to convey the true 'feel' of a Viking sea-battle. It is an extract from the saga's account of the Battle of Svöldr, describing the closing moments of the conflict after Olaf's ship, the giant *Long Serpent*, had been surrounded by those of his enemies, including Earl Eric Hakonsson of Lade in the *Iron Beard*:

'Earl Eric was in the forehold of his ship, where a shield-wall had been set up. Hewing weapons—the sword and axe—and thrusting spears alike were being used in the fighting, and everything that could be used as a missile was being thrown. Some shot with bows, others hurled javelins. In fact so many weapons rained down on the *Serpent*, so thickly flew the spears and arrows, that the shields could scarcely withstand them, for the *Serpent* was surrounded by longships on every side. At this King Olaf's men became so enraged that they ran on board the enemies' ships so as to have their attackers within reach of their swords and kill them. But many of the enemy ships had kept out of the *Serpent*'s reach so as to avoid this, and most of Olaf's men therefore fell

11th- or 12th-century nasal helmet, typical of those in use throughout Scandinavia and Western Europe during the preceding 200 years. Some 10th- and 11th-century Viking examples had copper and silver decoration to the eyebrow ridges and nasals; one example of this style has been excavated in Gotland, and it has been suggested that the so-called 'helmet of St Wenceslas' in Prague Cathedral, dating to the 10th century, is another. (Kunsthistorischen Museum, Vienna)

overboard and sank under the weight of their weapons.

'Einar Tambarskelve, one of the sharpest of archers, stood by the mast, shooting his bow. He shot an arrow at Earl Eric which hit the tiller-end just above his head so hard that it penetrated up to its shaft. The earl looked round and asked if anyone had seen who fired, just as another arrow flew between his hand and his side and sank so far into the head-board that its head came out on the other side. Then the earl said to a man called Fin (or who was a Finn, and an expert archer), "Shoot that tall man by the mast." Fin fired, and his arrow hit the middle of Einar's bow just as he was drawing it, and split it in two. "What was that, that broke with such a noise?" called King Olaf. "Norway, king," cried Einar, "from your grip."

'Desperate was the defence of the *Serpent*,

57

Shipwrights at work on the construction of the Norman fleet at the mouth of the River Dives in 1066, as depicted in the Bayeux Tapestry. The absence of saws in this picture supports the opinion of most archaeologists that, since there are no signs at all of saw-marks on the timbers of excavated ships, Viking shipwrights used only such tools as axes, adzes, planes, gouges, augers and draw-knives.

and the heaviest loss of life was inflicted by the defenders of the forecastle and forehold, for all of them were picked men and the ship's sides were highest there; but those defending the middle of the ship had been thinned, and when Earl Eric saw how few remained around the ship's mast he boarded there with 14 men. But Hyrning, the king's brother-in-law, came against them with some others and there was a stiff fight, at the end of which the earl was forced to leap back aboard the *Iron Beard*, some of those who had followed him having been killed and others wounded.

'Now the fighting became really intense on all sides; many aboard the *Serpent* were killed, and her defenders were thinned yet further. The earl decided to reboard the *Serpent* and again met with a warm reception. The forecastle men, seeing what he was doing, fell aft and made a desperate fight of it, but by now so many of the *Serpent*'s defenders had fallen that in places the ship's sides were entirely undefended, so that the earl's men were able to pour in on all sides. The surviving crew then crowded aft to protect the king.

'The battle was still raging even in the forehold, but there were by now as many of the

earl's men on board the *Serpent* as could find room and his ships lay all round her. There were nowhere near enough defenders left to repel so great a number, and before long most of the *Serpent*'s men had been killed, brave and stout though they were. Finally King Olaf and Kolbjorn the marshal both leapt overboard, one on each side. But the earl's men had set out their ship's boats all round the *Serpent* and were killing those who leaped overboard. These men tried to seize the king in order to take him to Earl Eric, but King Olaf threw his shield above his head and sank beneath the surface.'

F: A strandhögg

When the need arose to replenish a longship's stores the Vikings would indulge in a *strandhögg*, a shore-raid in which cattle and sheep were rounded up and either slaughtered, or taken aboard ship alive to provide fresh meat at a later date. Anti-social as this was, it had once been customary usage even in Scandinavia itself, where a man could feel free to help himself anywhere outside his own locale. However, in the 9th century, as larger portions of the North became unified under powerful kings, the custom fell into disfavour and perpetrators were outlawed (as, for instance, was Gange-Hrolf, Hrolf 'the Walker', founder of the duchy of Normandy). Overseas, revictualling continued to depend on 'strandhewing', which was also an excuse for rounding up young women and healthy youths for the thriving slave-trade, and for relieving the locals of whatever gold or valuables they had failed to hide

10th-century silver Thor's Hammer amulet from Fossi, Iceland. The similarity of shape between Thor's Hammers and crucifixes eased the conversion of pagan Vikings to Christianity in the 10th and 11th centuries. Denmark was officially converted in the mid-10th century; and Norway, Iceland, Orkney, the Faroes and Greenland all became Christian—often at the point of the sword—during the reign of Olaf Tryggvasson (995–1000). In parts of Sweden, however, the old religion continued to thrive until well into the 12th century, when the great pagan shrine at Uppsala was finally destroyed. (National Museum of Iceland, Reykjavik)

in time. The tall round-tower in the background—built as a refuge against such Viking raids—identifies the shore-raid depicted here as taking place in Ireland; in the foreground a slain bishop is being relieved of his gold and ivory crozier.

G: Eastern Vikings
Viking traders and warriors travelling in the East inevitably adopted, and brought back with them to Scandinavia, assorted Slavic and Central Asian modes of dress and weapons, as these figures clearly testify. Figure G1 is a *Rus* warrior, based predominantly on the descriptions set down by

Bronze statuette of Thor—god of the sky and the storm, yet the friend of mortal men—with his hammer Mjöllnir; from Eyjafjord in northern Iceland, this probably dates to about 1000. Thor and his father Odin were the chief gods of Scandinavian mythology, and in wartime an enemy might be formally dedicated to destruction as an offering to Odin, the 'gatherer of slain men'; this was normally done by a spear being hurled over their heads at the commencement of battle. (National Museum of Iceland, Reykjavik)

10th-century Arab and Byzantine writers, especially that of Leo the Deacon. His justly famous portrait of Svyatoslav, prince of Kiev 962–972, runs as follows: 'He was of medium height, with a powerful neck, a broad chest and a luxurious moustache. His nose was blunt, his eyes blue, his eyebrows bushy and his head shaven except for a lock of hair on either side, a token of his noble birth. In one ear he wore a silver ring decorated with two pearls and between them a carbuncle. His white tunic differed from his men's only by being cleaner.' Elsewhere he describes *Rus* arms as including tall shields 'the height of a man' (in fact they would have been about four feet tall) plus swords, bows, spears and javelins. In addition many wore mail corselets. The baggy trousers worn by this figure are based on warriors depicted in the Gotland picture

stones, and confirmed by the accounts of Arab travellers, who speak of the Russians wearing trousers 'of 100 spans' which they drew tight and fastened at the knees. Figure G2 also wears such trousers, while the rest of his equipment displays considerable Central Asian influence, including Magyar-style horse harness. He is based on a reconstruction by Bertil Almgren in *The Viking* (published by Nordbok), which is based in turn on assorted archaeological finds, notably from Birka in Sweden, an important centre for Viking trade in the East until *c*.980.

The background figures are Varangian Guardsmen of the 11th century, displaying the two attributes for which they were justly famous—their axes and their drinking. There are a number of anecdotes on record of drunken Varangians, and in

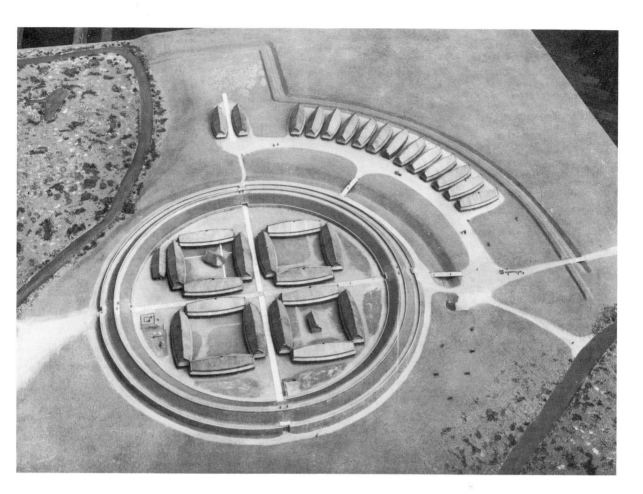

Aerial view and reconstruction of Trelleborg. For a full description see the caption to Plate H. (Nationalmuseet, Copenhagen)

1103 King Eric of Denmark, visiting Constantinople, exhorted members of the Guard to 'endeavour to lead a sober life and not give themselves up to drunkenness'. A 12th-century description of the Varangians as the Emperor's 'wine-bags' would therefore seem to be well-deserved.

H: *Trelleborg military camp, Denmark*

Trelleborg is one of four similar late 10th- or early 11th-century Danish military camps, which are thought to have been constructed as troop assembly points for Swein Forkbeard's operations against England, as they were apparently occupied only briefly (probably for a period not exceeding 80–90 years). Protected on three sides by rivers and a marsh, Trelleborg's principal man-made defences comprised a deep moat on the landward side, and a stockaded rampart, pierced by four gates at the compass points; from these gates roads divided the area within the rampart into four equal sectors, each containing four principal buildings arranged in squares. In addition there were a further 15 houses in the outer ward. The diameter of the camp area within the rampart was some 136 metres, with the rampart itself being about 17.5 metres thick and nearly seven metres high. The barracks were each nearly 30 metres long (those in the outer ward were slightly smaller), with a large middle room and a smaller room at each end; they could house some 40–50 men apiece. The camp was seemingly self-sufficient, apparently farming the adjacent fields and even having its own graveyard (top left); and at least some women appear to have lived there. H2 is a reconstruction of one of the boat-shaped barracks.

The other three similar known camps are at Nonnebakken on Funen, and at Fyrkat and Aggersborg in Jutland. The first two are much like Trelleborg, each with 16 houses similarly arranged, but Aggersborg is considerably larger, being some 287.5 metres in diameter, with 12 slightly bigger houses (32.5 metres long) in each sector instead of only four. Archaeological evidence indicates that these fortresses were all constructed between 970–1020, while we know that Aggersborg was destroyed during a revolt of 1086. Between them they could have housed a standing army of some 5,500 men.

I: A battle between Vikings and Skraelings

As well as colonising both Iceland and Greenland the Vikings also discovered America, which they called Vinland, in about 986, some 500 years before Columbus. At the beginning of the 11th century they established short-lived colonies in Newfoundland—at L'Anse aux Meadows—and, probably, in Labrador. Although evidence is sketchy, it would seem that occasional expeditions from Greenland continued thereafter until at least the 14th century, apparently for timber, which was in extremely short supply in Greenland; indeed, the Vikings actually called one part of Vinland by the name Markland ('Forestland'), and this is usually identified with the coast of Labrador.

The principal reason for the failure of their attempts at permanent settlement was clearly the

12th-century Viking warrior, from carvings on the stave church at Hylestad, Norway, depicting the legend of Sigurd the Dragon-Slayer. Note that a kite-shield has at last replaced the traditional circular one. His helmet has both nasal and neck-guard.

hostility of the *Skraelings* ('Wretches' or 'Screechers'), as the sagas call the Indians and Eskimoes alike. *Eirik's Saga* records how, after a skirmish with them in which two Norsemen and four Skraelings were killed, the leader of one expedition realised 'that although the land was excellent they could never live there in safety or freedom from fear, because of the native inhabitants. So they made ready to leave the place and return home.' From the sagas we know that these Skraelings were dark-skinned, with 'untidy, coarse hair', large eyes and broad cheeks; they were armed with slings, and quartzite- and flint-headed spears and arrows; were dressed in skins; and attacked the Viking ships with flotillas of skin canoes. Anthropologists have tentatively identified them with the extinct Micmac or Beothuk Indians, related to the Algonquins. The Skraelings responsible for the eventual extinction of the Greenland settlements were Eskimoes rather than Indians.

J: Late Vikings

These three figures bear witness to the gradual evolution of Scandinavian military equipment in the course of the 12th century, which brought it into line with that now employed throughout mainland Europe. J1 is a Hebridean, from the Lewis chess pieces of *c.*1175; J2 is a Norwegian, from the Baldishol tapestry of *c.*1180; and J3 is an Icelander, from the carved wooden doors of Valthjofsstadir Church, *c.*1200. It can be seen that conventional long 'kite' shields had by now replaced the old traditional round type; and that mail armour was in general use amongst the new knightly warrior caste that had begun to evolve under Western influence. Nevertheless, more often than not, sea-battles were still fought from longships in the time-honoured fashion, and land-battles were still fought on foot by close-packed men armed with sword, axe and spear as in earlier times. Indeed, in the sagas, which were first being set down in writing at about this time, there is absolutely no difference between descriptions of battles fought in the 10th century and those fought in the 12th. Scandinavian warriors may now have dressed like knights, and Christianity may have done something to reduce their savagery; but at heart they were still undeniably Vikings.

Further reading

There is a vast quantity of books generally available covering every aspect of Viking history, society and art. The following brief listing is restricted to those which the author found to be of the greatest value during the course of his research:

Bertil Almgren (Ed), *The Viking*, 1975; Holger Arbman, *The Vikings*, 1961; Ian Atkinson, *The Viking Ships*, 1980; Johannes Brøndsted, *The Vikings*, 1971; P. B. du Chaillu (Trans), *The Viking Age*, 1889; Frank R. Donovan, *The Vikings*, 1970; R. T. Farrell (Ed), *The Vikings*, 1982; G. N. Garmonsway (Trans), *The Anglo-Saxon Chronicle*, 1975; Michael Gibson, *The Vikings*, 1972; Helge Ingstad, *Westward to Vinland*, 1974; Gwyn Jones, *A History of the Vikings*, 1968; T. D. Kendrick, *A History of the Vikings*, 1968; Ole Klindt-Jensen, *The World of the Vikings*, 1970; Samuel Laing (Trans), *Heimskringla* (3 volumes), 1961–1964; H. R. Loyn, *The Vikings in Britain*, 1977; Magnus Magnusson, *Viking Expansion Westwards*, 1979; Magnus Magnusson and Hermann Pálsson (Trans), *Njal's Saga*, 1971, and *The Vinland Sagas: The Norse Discovery of America*, 1965; Eric Oxenstierna, *The Norsemen*, 1966; P. H. Sawyer, *The Age of the Vikings*, 1971; Jacqueline Simpson, *Everyday Life in the Viking Age*, 1967; J. H. Todd (Trans), *The War of the Gaedhil with the Gaill*, 1867; D. M. Wilson, *The Vikings and their Origins*, 1971; D. M. Wilson and P. G. Foote, *The Viking Achievement*, 1970; Michael Wood, *In Search of the Dark Ages*, 1981.

Another of the Lewis chessmen, this time a mounted knight in a conical helmet with nasal, earguards and neckguard. The Viking warrior was now almost indistinguishable from the fighting man of any Western European community—the *miles*, forerunner of the man-at-arms. (The Trustees of the British Museum)

Notes sur les planches en couleur

A, B: Divers costumes et armes Viking des 9e–11e siècles. Le costume de base comprenait une tunique à manches longues atteignant la cuisse ou le genou, portée sur une chemise; les pantalons étaient parfois étroits, parfois larges, parfois au genou avec des jambières séparées. Les chaussures et les bottes étaient en cuir, avec ou sans poils, comportant parfois des semelles en bois. Des capes courtes et parfois à la hanche; ils étaient faits dans de nombreux tissus, allant de la laine fine à une étoffe grossière et à poils et ils étaient parfois doublés de fourrure. De nombreuses couleurs étaient utilisées; le rouge, le vert et le bleu étaient populaires et un tissu à rayures est décrit dans certaines sources. Des bandes et des panneaux rapportés en broderie fine étaient communs. Les hommes étaient fiers de leur apparence, et particulièrement de leurs longs cheveux et de leur longue barbe. Ils se lavaient et se changeaient souvent.

L'épée était l'arme la plus prestigieuse, mais la hache, la lance, le javelin et l'arc étaient aussi couramment portés. Le *skeggox* et le *breidox* (B2) étaient des types de hache typiques. Les Vikings furent responsables de la re-introduction de la hache de combat dans le reste de l'Europe à cette époque. Des boucliers en bois, parfois recouverts de cuir, avec bossage et bords en fer, étaient peints de couleurs unies (rouge, jaune, noir, blanc, et dans un moindre mesure, vert et bleu) ou avec des motifs mythiques. Il semble que la plupart des casques étaient d'un modèle conique simple. Les corselets de maille, réservés tout d'abord aux riches guerriers, devinrent plus répandus au 11e siècle, époque à laquelle les Vikings n'avaient pas un aspect très différent de celui de leurs contemporains anglo-saxons ou normands.

C: Le costume masculin semble n'avoir pas changé de façon fondamentale durant toute l'époque viking. Une longue chemise en laine ou en toile était recouverte de deux morceaux de tissu—dont la composition allait de la laine à la soie—attachés aux épaules par des broches, dont la qualité variait aussi. Les femmes mariées tressaient leurs cheveux ou les recouvraient d'un foulard alors que les jeunes filles les portaient lâches. Elles avaient les bras nus, par coquetterie, et des sources arabes semblent suggérer que le fard pour les yeux n'était pas inconnu.

D: Les bateaux étaient construits durant l'hiver, en chêne si ce matériau était disponible, ou en pin, en frêne, en bouleau, s'il ne l'était pas—mais la quille était toujours en chêne. La quille était construite en premier; l'étrave et l'étambot étaient ajoutés, puis le vaigrage et finalement les membrures qui n'étaient attachées au vaigrage que par des racines de sapin, ce qui donnait une flexibilité supérieure. **D1:** Gréage. **D2, D3:** Palan de montage pour le mât, qui pouvait être abaissé en mer. **D7:** Aviron de direction. **D4:** Support à boucliers. **D5:** Orifices pour avirons. **D6:** Aviron. **D8:** Vue en coupe dans la partie médiane du bateau trouvé à Gokstad.

E: Reconstitution d'une bataille navale. Celles-ci étaient conduites de façon très similaire à celle des batailles au sol. Les bateaux d'une flottille pouvaient même être rangés côte à côte pour former une large plateforme de combat qui était assaillie par les navires ennemis. Ce tableau est inspiré par la Saga du roi Olaf Tryggvason, qui décrit sa fin à la bataille de Svöldr en l'an 1000, lorsque son navire le 'Long Serpent' fut isolé et entouré par les navires de Jarl Eric Hakonsson. Il semble y avoir eu peu de tentatives pour défoncer ou détruire les avirons de l'ennemi avec la proue, tactique classique du monde grec et romain. Les batailles en mer étaient décidées simplement par abordage et combat corps-à-corps, après barrage par flèches, javelins et pierres.

F: Raid viking en Irlande, pour obtenir provisions, esclaves, et tout butin qui se présentait. A une certaine époque, ces raids étaient une pratique acceptée en Scandinavie mais ils furent désapprouvés par la suite—on considérait qu'il y avait tant de richesses à prendre à l'étranger! Gange-Hrolf, plus tard 'Duc Rollo de Normandie', fut mis hors la loi pour cette pratique.

G: Les coutumes des peuples slaves et d'Asie Centrale en matière d'habillement, d'armes et d'armure furent adoptées par les voyageurs vikings dans l'intérieur de la Russie et à Byzance. **G1:** Guerrier *Rus* d'après la description d'un témoin oculaire des Svyatoslaves de Kiev, vers 970. **G2:** Ce personnage porte des pantalons très larges, probablement d'origine russe, et un costume magyra. En arrière-plan, des gardes varangiens de l'armée byzantine—les gardes au bonnet en vigne de l'empereur.

H: On connaît quatre camps très similaires du 10e ou du début du 11e siècle, à Trelleborg, Nonnebakken, Fyrkat et Aggersborg; l'ensemble de ces casernes impressionnantes aurait pu loger plus de 5.000 hommes. On pense qu'ils ont été construits pour les opérations du roi Swein Forkbeard contre l'Angleterre.

I: Illustration basée sur les descriptions fragmentaires des *Skraelings*—les 'crieurs' dont les ambuscades et les raids constants convainquirent les vikings établis en Vinland (Terre-Neuve et Labrador) que leur établissement en Amérique n'avait pas d'avenir. D'après des descriptions dans la Saga d'Eirik et autres sources, les historiens pensent que les 'crieurs' étaient les indiens Micmac ou Beothuk, dont la race est maintenant éteinte.

J: L'évolution du guerrier viking en guerrier européen. **J1:** D'après un jeu d'échecs sculpté trouvé sur l'île de Lewis. **J2:** D'après la tapisserie de Baldishol. **J3:** D'après la porte d'église sculptée de Valthjofsstadir. Datant tous d'entre 1175 à 1200 approximativement.

Farbtafeln

A, B: Eine Reihe Vikinger-Uniformen und Waffen aus dem 9.–11. Jahrhundert. Die Grunduniform bestand aus einer langärmeligen Tunika, die bis zum Schenkel bzw. Knie reichte und über dem Hemd getragen wurde. Die Hosen waren manchmal eng, manchmal weit und reichten zuweilen bis ans Knie mit Gamaschen. Schuhe und Stiefel waren aus Leder, auf dem manchmal noch Fell war. Einige Schuhe hatten Holzsohlen. Die Vikinger trugen sowohl kurze Capes als auch lange Umhänge, die entweder an der rechten Schulter oder an der Hüfte befestigt wurden. Hierfür verwendeten sie viele verschiedene Materialien, von feiner Wolle bis zu rauhem, borstigem Material, und manchmal Fell als Futter. Unter vielen Farben waren rot, grün und blau besonders populär; manche Kleidungsstücke waren laut Überlieferungen sogar gestreift. Gestickte Borten und Bordüren waren üblich. Die Vikinger waren sehr eitel, besonders was ihr langes Haar und ihre Bärte anging. Sie wechselten und wuschen häufig ihre Kleidung.

Das Schwert war die beliebteste Waffe, aber sie trugen häufig auch Äxte, Speere, Lanzen und Bogen. Typische Äxte dieser Zeit waren die *Skeggox* und die *Breidox* (B2). Zu dieser Zeit führten die Vikinger die Streitaxt wieder in restlichen Europa ein. Ihre Holz- oder mit Leder bezogenen Schilder mit Buckeln und Umrandungen aus Metall bemalten sie mit simplen Farben (rot, gelb, schwarz, weiss oder auch seltener grün und blau) oder mit mythischen Motiven. Die meisten Helme schienen eine einfache konische Form zu haben. Kettenhemden wurden zunächst nur von reicheren Kriegern getragen, aber im 11. Jahrhundert waren sie schon sehr verbreitet, und ein Vikingerkrieger unterschied sich kaum von seinem angelsächsischen oder normannischen Gegner.

C: Die Damenbekleidung blieb die ganze Vikingerzeit hindurch fast unverändert: ein langes Hemd aus Leinen oder Wolle wurde von zwei Bekleidungsstücken—aus Material von Wolle bis Seide—bedeckt und an den Schultern mit unterschiedlich kostbaren Broschen befestigt. Verheiratete Frauen flochten ihr Haar oder trugen Kopftücher, während junge Mädchen ihr Haar offen trugen. Unbedeckte Arme waren ein Zeichen von Eitelkeit. Einer arabischen Überlieferung zufolge kannten die Vikingerfrauen sogar Augenmakeup.

D: Im Winter wurden Schiffe gebaut, entweder aus Eiche, falls vorhanden, oder aus Kiefer, Esche, Birke usw., aber der Kiel war immer aus Eiche. Den Kiel fertigte man zuerst. Später kamen Vorder- und Achtersteven hinzu, dann die Beplankung und schliesslich die Schiffsrippen, die nur mit Fichtenwurzeln an der Beplankung festgebunden wurden und das Schiff daher sehr flexibel machten. **D1:** Takelage. **D2, D3:** Aufstellen des Blocks für den Mast, den man auf dem Meer herunterlassen konnte. **D7:** Steuerruder. **D4:** Schildgestell. **D5:** Ruderluken. **D6:** Ruder. **D8:** Teilansicht der Mitte des Schiffs, das bei Gokstad gefunden wurde.

E: Eine Seeschlacht, die wie eine Landschlacht ausgefochten wurde. Schiffe einer Flotte wurden sogar gelegentlich nebeneinander gebunden, um eine breite Kampffläche zu formen, die feindlichen Schiffe dann stürmten. Das Gemälde beruht wahrscheinlich auf der Sage von König Olaf Tryggvason und beschreibt sein Ende in der Schlacht von Svöldr im Jahre 1000 AD, als sein Schiff, die 'Lange Schlange' abgeschnitten und von den Schiffen Jarl Erik Hakonssons umzingelt wurde. Man schien keinerlei Versuche zu unternehmen, die feindlichen Ruder mit dem Bug zu rammen oder zu zerschmettern, was die bei den Griechen und Römern übliche Taktik war. Seeschlachten wurden ganz einfach durch Pfeile, Speere und Steine und durch Entern und offene Kämpfe entschieden.

F: Die Vikinger überfallen Irland, um Provision, Sklaven und andere Beute einzunehmen. Es gab eine Zeit, da galten solche Überfälle in Skandinavien als Gang und Gäbe; später erst wurden sie kritisiert—schliesslich gab es im Ausland genügend zu holen! Gange-Hrolf, der spätere 'Herzog Rollo von der Normandie' wurde hierfür verbannt.

G: Vikinger, die in das russische Hinterland und nach Byzanz reisten, übernahmen slavische und mittelasiatische Kleidungsstücke, Waffen und Rüstungen. **G1:** Ein *Rus*-Krieger gemäss Augenzeugenberichten über Svyatoslav von Kiev um c.a. 970. **G2:** Trägt die sehr weite Hose, die wahrscheinlich aus Russland stammt, sowie Magyar-Kleidung. Im Hintergrund die Varangianische Garde der Byzantinischen Armee—'die Weinschläuche des Kaisers'.

H: Vier sehr ähnliche Lager aus dem 10. oder frühen 11. Jahrhundert sind bekannt: Trelleborg, Nonnebaken, Fyrkat und Aggersborg. Diese Lager konnten zusammen über 5000 Krieger beherbergen. Sie wurden vermutlich für König Swein Forkbeards Feldzug gegen England erbaut.

I: Sie basieren auf den wenigen Beschreibungen der *Skraelings*—der 'Kreischer', deren häufige Überfälle und Hinterhalte die Vikingersiedler in Vinland (Neufundland und Labrador) überzeugten, dass es für sie in Amerika keine Zukunft gab. Gemäss der Beschreibung in der Eirik Sage und anderen Quellen behaupten Historiker, die 'Kreischer' seien Angehörige der ausgerotteten Micmac und Beothuk-Indianer.

J: Entwicklung der Vikinger zu europäischen Kriegern. **J1:** Gemäss einem geschnitzten Schachspiel, einem Fund auf der Insel Lewis. **J2:** Gemäss der Baldishol-Tapisserie. **J3:** Von der geschnitzten Tür der Valthjofsstadir-Kirche. Alle stammen aus der Zeit zwischen c.a. 1175 und 1200.